A BOOK OF GREEK LIFE

GIDEON NISBET

A BOOK OF GREEK LIFE

The Ancient World Through Epigram

OXFORD
UNIVERSITY PRESS

Great Clarendon Street, Oxford, OX2 6DP,
United Kingdom

Oxford University Press is a department of the University of Oxford.
It furthers the University's objective of excellence in research, scholarship,
and education by publishing worldwide. Oxford is a registered trade mark of
Oxford University Press in the UK and in certain other countries.

Links to third party websites are provided by Oxford in good faith and
for information only. Oxford disclaims any responsibility for the materials
contained in any third party website referenced in this work.

Published in the United States of America by Oxford University Press
198 Madison Avenue, New York, NY 10016, United States of America

British Library Cataloguing in Publication Data
Data available

Library of Congress Control Number: 2026937369

ISBN 9780198994756

DOI: 10.1093/oso/9780198994756.001.0001

Printed and bound by
CPI Group (UK) Ltd., Croydon, CR0 4YY

The manufacturer's authorized representative in the EU for product safety is
Oxford University Press España S.A. of Parque Empresarial San Fernando de Henares,
Avenida de Castilla, 2 – 28830 Madrid (www.oup.es/en or product.safety@oup.com).
OUP España S.A. also acts as importer into Spain of products made by the manufacturer.

CONTENTS

INTRODUCTION

This is a book of Greek life. It is your book, who hold it in your hands, and mine, who made it, but it is a hand-me-down. Its tiny poems, called *epigrams*, are a small fraction of a much bigger and older book called the Greek Anthology. This great compendium of around four thousand epigrams was compiled in Constantinople, the city we now call Istanbul, early in the tenth century of the Christian era; not 'ancient' as ancient historians would reckon it, but still well over a thousand years ago.

Rome had fallen nearly half a millennium before (AD 476), but the city on the Bosporus refounded by Constantine, the first Christian-adjacent Emperor, continued to flourish as the capital of the surviving eastern half of the Roman Empire. Its citizens proudly called themselves Romans, though they said it in Greek—**Rhōmaioi**. They worshipped the Christian God and had given up on gladiators, but they kept their consuls and chariot races. The palace was a maze of plots and bureaucratic manoeuvring (we call such things 'Byzantine' for a reason), but the eastern Empire had always been rich and cultured and in the tenth century it was again militarily triumphant. Its capital city combined every-thing that was most gripping about the cultures of Greece and

A Book of Greek Life: The Ancient World Through Epigram. Gideon Nisbet, Oxford University Press.
© Gideon Nisbet 2026. DOI: 10.1093/oso/9780198994756.003.0001

Rome alike—philosophy and rhetoric, bread and circuses—and husbanded the wisdom of its classical forebears. Byzantium's intellectual resources were so great that when the city fell to the Turks five centuries later (1453) the westward trickle of refugee knowledge from its wreckage helped kickstart the Renaissance.

In this cosmopolis a scholar named Constantine Cephalas undertook an awesome project of antiquarianism. Trawling the city's marvellous libraries, he sought to assemble and organize whatever survived of a whole ancient genre, epigram. There were some obvious choices: poets and researchers had been collecting epigrams since before the birth of Christ, and Cephalas leaned heavily on ancient predecessors. The earliest of these, Meleager of Gadara (first century BC) and Philip of Thessalonica (first century AD), had called their collections *Garlands*; literally in Greek the work of the anthologist is to gather flowers (**anthē**), and the work of a great **antho**-logist was to weave those blooms into something beautiful, more than the sum of its parts.

Cephalas' huge new Anthology was not beautiful at all. He was not aiming to select and titivate, but to safeguard the whole lot for posterity. He dug around, pulling old elegiac epitaphs out of, for instance, Herodotus. The famous 'Go tell the Spartans, passer-by...' is one such, written by Simonides to inscribe on the monument to the three hundred Spartiates who fell at Thermopylae facing the massed armies of Xerxes of Persia. As it happens we still have Herodotus, but Cephalas was taking no chances.

Epigram and the Anthology

Epigrams are simply short poems, often collected. Each is complete in and of itself, though its meaning is enriched by the poems that come before and after in space (on paper, on stone) and time. They were typically written in a rhythm or *metre* called *elegiac couplets*, consisting of a *hexameter* (a line of six metrical units) and a shorter *pentameter* (a line of five), but not always. Ancient and mediaeval manuscripts and modern printed editions signal this by indenting each pentameter line. There can be one couplet, two, three, or occasionally more. One consequence is that however long or short they may be, all elegiac epigrams have an even number of lines. Regardless of the metres of the originals, my versions just go di-dum, di-dum, di-dum. Epigrams in the English literary tradition (Ben Jonson and such) are usually satirical and end with a punchline, but the influence there is a racy Latin epigrammatist called Martial; Greek epigrams mostly don't do that.

What are the epigrams of the Greek Anthology about? Almost anything, and that is the joy of them. In this comparatively small sample you will find poems about gods, monsters, lovers and courtesans, thinkers and makers, pets, pirates, schoolchildren, scholars and soldiers, and the everyday trades and agricultural labour that kept the whole thing going. These aren't 'historical documents', they're better than that: the Anthology opens countless little windows into ancient experience and imagination.

Who wrote those epigrams? Almost anybody who could write, or who might be invited to a *symposium*, the traditional after-dinner drinking party at which Greek men entertained each other and expressed their shared values. As far as we know we have no epigrams by slaves or children or labourers, but poets such as Anyte and Nossis open up horizons of women's experience—though these women poets also take an interest in what we might have taken for men's business, including war. And epigrams could be written about and for almost anyone, slaves, labourers, and children included. Epigram became a form of literature in the years after Alexander the Great, but it had begun centuries earlier as genuine verse inscriptions that let stones speak, and the occasions for such inscriptions never went away. Archaeologists find epigrams cut into statue-bases and monuments, offerings and tombs, including the tombs of perfectly ordinary people.

The study of excavated *papyri* (**5.9**), of which the most important recent discovery is a near-complete *book-roll* (scroll) by the early poet Posidippus now in Milan (**5.147**), confirms that ancient authors of books of epigram usually arranged their poems into headed categories—epitaphs, dedications, love-poems, and so on. Almost every anthologist followed suit. The process is writ large in the Greek Anthology, each big book of which (with a few odd exceptions) collects epigrams of a particular kind. Cephalas built it to be useful, and rather than try to be artistic I adopt its structure here.

The poems within each book are numbered, and each bears a descriptive heading (called a *lemma*) that tells us who wrote it, more reliably than not. We navigate the Anthology by book number plus poem number. Simonides' 'Go tell the Spartans' for instance is 7.249, the 249th poem of Book 7. If you explore epigram beyond *A Book of Greek Life* you will see those numbers prefixed with the letters AP, short for *Anthologia Palatina*, the Palatine Anthology. You don't *need* to know what that is, but you can read about it at **13.2–6** if you like.

For reference, here is what the whole thing looks like. It's a bit of a jumble, the front end especially:

1. Christian epigrams;
2. Cyzicene epigrams;

3. An epic by Christodorus of Coptic Thebes (who?) describing works of art;

4. The prefaces to the anthologies that came before;

5. **Erotic epigrams**;

6. **Dedicatory epigrams**;

7. **Funerary epigrams**;

8. The epigrams of Gregory of Nazianzus;

9. **Epideictic epigrams**;

10. **Advisory epigrams**;

11. Sympotic and satirical epigrams;

12. **Homoerotic epigrams ('Strato's Boyish Muse')**;

13. **Polymetric epigrams**;

14. **Puzzles and riddles**;

15. **Miscellaneous**;

16. The Planudean Appendix.

This book and how to read it

If you don't know what half those words mean (*'epideictic?'*), don't panic—you'll find out what you need to know along the way in easy stages, and half of them won't be your problem anyway. *A Book of Greek Life* samples just the books in bold. The rest are left out for various reasons: they're all about God (Book 1), or all by one person (Book 8), or from one site (Book 2), or aren't a book of the original Anthology (Book 16), or don't contain epigrams at all (Books 3 and 4). There is not much from Book 10, and nothing at all from Book 11: these two are so full of good stuff that they would fill a whole other book. More than half of the Anthology is plenty to be getting on with. We wrap up with two poems that Meleager used to conclude his own *Garland*.

Each translated epigram (or two, or three) cues up a page or two of discussion—somewhere between a blurb and a mini-essay—about some aspect or aspects of how the ancient world worked...or how people back then *imagined* it worked...or sometimes how people since then have tried to *pretend* it worked. The topics range widely. You will pick up a handful of italicized terms of art, a scattering of etymologies, and some insights into how we know what we know (and also what we *don't* know). You will also get a sense of how personal and passionate scholarship can be, however dusty it may sometimes look from outside: the ancient world is awesomely weird and so are a lot of the people who study it. Think twice before you lend this book to your kids. The whole of the ancient world should carry a trigger warning for, well, *everything*.

The translations were made for this book, many of them by way of an academic blog which you can find easily thanks to my unusual name. Others I made for my students or for presentations at conferences. The discussions that follow them sometimes give additional examples; if their identifying numbers are in **bold**, they too are newly made for this book. The remaining few are borrowed from my World's Classics translation, *Epigrams from the Greek Anthology* (2020). There's no need to start at the beginning and work though, though you certainly can do that. This is a book made with bus-rides and bathrooms in mind, and it's meant to be fun, so by all means dip in and out. There are lots of cross-connections and threads for you to follow—references to poems and discussions elsewhere in the book are again in **bold**.

Words transcribed from the Greek are also in **bold**, and Latin ones (along with some classics jargon) in *italics*. Vowels that end Greek words are pronounced long; I mark some others that are meant to bē tāken slōwly, thus. Sometimes I refer to letters of the Greek alphabet; here it is for reference, from alpha to ōmega:

A, α	alpha	a
B, β	bēta	b
Γ, γ	gamma	g
Δ, δ	delta	d
E, ϵ	epsilon	short e ('met')
Z, ζ	zēta	z (sd, shifting later to ds)
H, η	ēta	long e ('fair')
I, ι	iōta	short i ('hit')
K, κ	kappa	k
Λ, λ	lambda	l
M, μ	mu	m
N, ν	nu	n
Ξ, ξ	xi	x
O, o	omicron	short o ('hot')
Π, π	pi	p
P, ρ	rhō	r (a rolled r)
$\Sigma, \sigma/s$	sigma	s
T, τ	tau	t
Y, υ	upsilon	u
Φ, φ	phi	ph
X, χ	chi	ch ('loch')
Ψ, ψ	psi	ps
Ω, ω	ōmega	long o ('home')

The **mikron** and **psilon** in some of those letter-names mean 'small' and 'light', and the **mega** in ōmega means big (a megalith is a big stone; a microscope is for looking at small stuff). Iota (I) is the littlest letter to write, which is why some people don't care one iota, and pi you know from maths. There's no Q or W, and no C, just a K; that Z comes between the two Es takes a bit of getting used to; remembering which of phi, chi, and psi is which, takes more. The shapes of the capital letters are well fitted to cutting into surfaces such as stone; the small ones came later and suit a reed pen. The twenty-four letters are also numbers (this will come up later), and the Greeks divided the epics of Homer into twenty-four books, numbering them *A* to *Ω*, because somewhere in them was everything a person needed to know.

The word 'alphabet' comes from the first two letters of the Greek one. The alphabet we use today grew out of one the Romans adapted from Greek colonists in Italy, so it's not so very different, but isn't the Greek one prettier? It's also great for writing down things you don't want other people to know. Search online for '*Polar Record* Greek penguins' if you want to be put off your lunch.

Why 'a book of Greek life'?

A hundred and fifty years ago, John Addington Symonds wrote of epigram that,

> If we might compare the study of Greek literature to a journey in some splendid mountain region, then we might say with propriety that from the sparkling summits where Aeschylus and Sophocles and Pindar sit enthroned we turn in our less strenuous

moods to gather the meadow flowers of Meleager, Palladas, Callimachus....

They treat with a touching limpidity and sweetness of the joys and fears and hopes and sorrows that are common to all humanity. They introduce us to the actual life of a bygone civilization, stripped of its political or religious accidents, and tell us that the Greeks of Athens or of Sidon thought and felt exactly as we feel. Even the *Graffiti* of Pompeii have scarcely more power to reconstruct the past and summon as in dreams the voices and the forms of long-since-buried men.

Symonds dubbed the Anthology 'the book of Greek life', and my title nods to him. The first great salesman of Greek literature in the trade press, he made epigram the climax of his story, and he was right about its appeal—the Anthology went on to generate decades of controversy and delight, though it has since faded from popular memory. This book aims to give it a fresh chance to amuse and inform readers who are curious about the ancient world.

How to go further

If you catch the epigram bug, you will find an out-of-copyright translation of the whole thing for free online. Search for 'Loebolus' and grab PDFs of this and other ancient treasures to your heart's content. The Loeb *Greek Anthology* in five volumes was made by W. R. Paton in the 1910s; it is a heroic labour, packed with learning. Or there's my World's Classics selection *Epigrams from the Greek Anthology*, if you like what I do with epigram and want a bigger helping. In the meantime, please enjoy exploring the reality and imagination of long-ago lives that are uncannily like *and* unlike our own. In we go.

Timeline of main poets and anthologists

Sixth to fifth century BC

Simonides

Third century BC

Asclepiades
Callimachus
Dioscorides
Hedylus
Leonidas of Tarentum
Mnasalcas
Posidippus
Theocritus

Second century BC

Antipater of Sidon

First century BC

Archias
Gaetulicus
Meleager (*Garland*)
Philodemus

First century BC–first century AD

Antipater of Thessalonica

Crinagoras
Marcus Argentarius
Leonidas of Alexandria

First century AD

Lucillius
Nicarchus
Philip (*Garland*)
Rufinus?
Strato

Second century AD

Diogenian (*Anthologion*)
Lucian

Fourth century AD

Palladas
Gregory of Nazianzus 'the Theologian'

Sixth century AD

Agathias (*Cycle*)
Julian, Prefect of Egypt
Macedonius the Consul
Paul the Silentiary

THE LOVE POEMS

5.7 Asclepiades

Lamp, you were there when Heraclea swore
That she would come, and still she is not here.
She swore by you; so if you are a god,
Frustrate that lying woman. Every time
She entertains a caller, douse your flame,
And steal the lamplight from their indoor game.

Book 5 of the Anthology is full of erotic epigrams. It would be a stretch to call them love poems; they are about **erōs**, sexual desire, in this case for the opposite sex. The perspective is almost exclusively male. Book 12, built around an ancient collection by Strato of Sardis called the *Boyish Muse*, contains the Anthology's poems of male same-sex desire. Like us, Greeks and Romans acknowledged that individual tastes differed and might change over time. They did not tend to think of sexuality as an identity in the way that we do—indeed they had no word for 'identity', which seems to be a fairly recent concept. Some poets wrote about pretty young men and women interchangeably, including

A Book of Greek Life: The Ancient World Through Epigram. Gideon Nisbet, Oxford University Press.
© Gideon Nisbet 2026. DOI: 10.1093/oso/9780198994756.003.0002

the most famous of all literary epigrammatists, Meleager of Gadara, a cultured town known to readers of the New Testament for its demonically possessed pigs (Mark 5.1–13) but rich in poets. Meleager compiled the first and most famous of the Anthology's ancient prototypes, the *Garland* (first century BC). The winnowing of gay and straight loves came much later, in Christian Byzantium.

Heraclea is late for her appointment. The ancient Greeks and Romans divided day and night into twelve equal hours apiece. Daylight hours were measured on sundials, like this one (**9.806**) in a suburban park, described by an unknown Christian poet, marking workday hours:

> . . .
> This very stone, erected here, proclaims
> Seven instalments of the wheeling sky
> That spins forever and inexorably.

Those few people who needed to keep track of night hours used devices such as water clocks. Any such mechanism needed constant adjustment, because in spring the hours of night grew shorter as the nights themselves contracted, while daylight hours grew longer; in autumn the situation was turned around.

Whatever the season, ancient cities had no street lighting and were very dark at night. People with legitimate reason to be out after dark (sex workers, police patrols, returning dinner-guests, forlorn lovers) found their way by torchlight; the interiors of houses and apartments were lit by tallow candles or clay oil-lamps. Candles were for the poor; lamps were nicer to live with, but olive oil was always in demand (for cosmetics and medicines as well as in kitchens and at table) and never cheap. Such lamps were typically mass-produced, stamped out in moulds, and the huge output meant lots of variety in shape and style. Many were decorated, some had more than one spout, and occasionally they were even personalized. Before its clay was fired, someone with access to a potter's workshop in fourth-century Sicily incised a motto around the hole in the top through which one particular lamp was to be filled with oil: 'I am Pausanias' most buggered hole.' It may be rude, but it scans as a line of poetry, making it a very short inscriptional epigram.

When erotic epigram emerged in the Hellenistic age it made the lamp a regular accomplice of lovers. Greeks and Romans were as turned on by looks as lovers are today, and liked to see what they were doing. Here is another such epigram (5.128) by a much later poet, Marcus Argentarius:

> Bosom to bosom, breast that leaned on breast,
> Lips clasped to lips of sweet Antigone;
> Flesh reaching out to flesh. I say no more
> Of what our confidant, the oil-lamp, saw.

And here, Meleager (**6.162**), thanking the goddess of love for granting him many successes:

> To you, friend Cypris, Meleager leaves
> His favourite lamp, the playmate in his games,
> Accomplice to your night-long revelries.

In Asclepiades' poem a male lover suspects that his sexual partner is with another man. She is a **hetaira**, literally a companion who makes her way in the world by entertaining male clients (**5.138**), but this does not stop the speaker being jealous—he had booked her for the evening and suspects she has taken a better offer, probably one that does not require her to cross the city at night. Everyone knew the streets were dangerous: Posidippus at **5.213**, waiting outside a lady's door, begs her maid to tell her:

> That I came tipsy through the midst of thieves,
> Trusting in reckless Erōs as my guide.

5.9 Rufinus

> *Rufinus to my Elpis the most sweet.*
> *I hope this letter finds you in good health,*
> If you can be in health with me away.
> I cannot touch my solitary girl
> And by my eyes I swear I cannot stand
> Our separation and my lonely bed,
> But damp with tears I climb Coressus' hill
> Or to the temple of great Artemis.
> Tomorrow, though, I will have come back home,
> To our own city, and to you will fly,
> *With all best wishes for your flourishing.*

Composed by a specialist in erotic epigram, this poetic love letter packs intense passion between standard formulae of greeting and farewell. Like their modern equivalents, ancient letters tended to open and close in predictable ways. We know this not just from the published correspondences of the great and good, notably Cicero and the younger Seneca and Pliny, but from a multitude of letters written by ordinary people.

These two kinds of letter reach us in two completely different ways. It is amazing to think that Cicero's letters, for instance, come down to us through an unbroken chain of manuscript copies stretching all the way back through the Renaissance, Middle Ages, late antiquity, and Empire to his own Roman Republic. It is equally wonderful that with archaeology we can read letters written by everyday men, women, and sometimes children who lived two millennia ago—but only letters that were sent to or within a single Roman province. They survive on *papyrus* (plural *papyri*), the standard paper of antiquity. Though it was used for letters and other documents all over the ancient world, as well as for making books of literature, papyrus was made only in Egypt, from the sliced and squashed stems of a reed that grows in the Nile. The study of ancient papyri is called *papyrology*, and you can find out what makes an *-ology* in the little essay that goes with epigram **5.10**. Papyrus grows in a few other places (and today you can get it as a houseplant from IKEA), but it was commercially harvested and turned into paper only in Egypt.

By sheer geographical coincidence Egypt is also the only place ancient papyri survive, for the completely separate reason that it's very dry there. (There are isolated exceptions to these sweeping statements—beechwood writing-tablets from Vindolanda on Hadrian's Wall, carbonized papyri from Herculaneum (**5.30**)—but those are other stories.) Modern excavation has brought many of these documents to light while raising difficult questions in relation to colonial exploitation (the gold-rush years of Egyptian archaeology were under the British 'Veiled Protectorate'); provenance (any collectible antiquity that lacks a secure chain of evidence is almost certainly grave-robbed and smuggled); and even authenticity, as in the case of the so-called Artemidorus Papyrus (which I think probably *is* genuine) and the infamous Gospel of Jesus's Wife (which definitely isn't).

The speaker of this poem writes to his girlfriend Elpis (Hope) from a port district of Ephesus, the paramount coastal city of what is now western Turkey. When it came under Roman control in the second century BC it was already eight hundred years old, and its great Temple of Artemis was recognized as a Wonder of the World (**6.10**). We aren't sure exactly where the Coressus district lay, but sources say it had a good harbour, with a hill behind. The harbour is important because there was no ancient postal service except for couriers of Roman state correspondence. Rufinus' letter needs to catch a ride with someone sailing in the right direction, though we don't know what that direction was, since we have no clear idea of where Rufinus came from or when he was writing—that is, if we choose to identify the poem's speaker with the flesh-and-blood Rufinus in the first place. Nobody was ever obliged to.

It is admittedly confusing that there are two Plinies and two Senecas, differentiated as Elder and Younger in each case. The Elder ones were hardcore, the Younger, wusses. Pliny the Elder wrote an Encyclopaedia of Everything and sailed a warship straight at Vesuvius (**5.120**) as it blew; invited to join him, his nephew stayed home and (by his own confession) did his homework.

5.10 Alcaeus \<of Messene\>

I hate the god of Love. For why not slake
His brutal urges on the savage beasts?
Why shoot his darts into my heart instead?
What profit for a god to burn a man

Till he is ashes? And what special prize
Can he have earned by handing in my head?

The tags in angle brackets <LIKE THIS> are not in the manuscript; classicists use them when we want to make it clear that we have added something likely or helpful into a text. In this case I have put them in to disambiguate Alcaeus the writer of epigram (third to second centuries BC) from Alcaeus of Lesbos (early sixth century), the famous lyric poet.

Cupid's bow and arrows are ancient in origin. The wicked winged child of Aphrodite, goddess of sex and marriage, Erōs (whom the Romans called *Cupido*) loosed shafts that caused fierce desire. This might be experienced as an inner fire, disease, poison, or a mix of all three. His choice of targets was famously capricious. For a love poet such as Alcaeus he is a professional hazard as well as an abundant source of material.

The poetic commonplace or *topos* of love as a sickness is already there in the archaic lyric of Sappho (the famous fr. 31, beginning 'He seems to me to equal to a god') but came into its own in the Hellenistic age, which saw the birth of literary epigram alongside rapid progress in understanding the processes that drive the human body. The new fascination with our own plumbing and wiring (**7.158**) echoes in new kinds of poetry emerging in the same time and place, for instance, in the biomechanics of Medea falling for Jason in the *Argonautica* of Apollonius of Rhodes. In the Museum of Alexandria poets rubbed shoulders with scientists, who might themselves sometimes turn poet: Eratosthenes, who calculated the circumference of the earth with fair accuracy, presented some of his mathematical findings to Ptolemy with an accompanying epigram.

When Aristotle wrote that 'man is a political animal', he put **anthrōpos**—humanity—as just another species of animal (**zōon**), alongside badgers and all the rest. The word lives on in modern words such as anthropoid and anthropomorphism. A misogynist hates women (**gunai**) and a misandrist, men (**andres**), but a misanthropist despises the whole human lot of us. Werewolves are lycanthropes, a blend of human and wolf (**lukos**), and that word is ancient. To know why we say lycanthropy and not lukanthropy, see **5.34**.

According to Aristotle the main thing that marks humans out from badgers etc. is the kind of nest we build: nature directs us to make cities, and gives us the ability to reason and talk (**logos**) so that we can form these complex communities. The Greek for city is **polis**, and *that* is what makes us a **politikon zōon**. The Greeks knew that in most ways we are animals just like all the rest, sharing their instincts and appetites, but they also saw that **logos** made our sexual relationships more complicated than those of other species, with lots of potentially messy consequences. 'Situationship', they call it now. Much of Greek myth is about very little else.

Alcaeus is the name of a very famous lyric poet, the contemporary and fellow-citizen of Sappho of Lesbos (**7.17**), but this is a different Alcaeus. He came from Messene in the south-eastern Peloponnese, and political references in his poems date him to the late third and early second centuries BC, about four hundred years after his Lesbian (but not lesbian) eponym. **Logos**, reason, is also the study of something so as to bring it into rational understanding; hence all our *-ologies*, which we only think of that way rather than as *-logies* because the Greek roots that precede the *-log* tend to end with an 'o'—anthropology and zoology, for two. And yes, **zōon** is also where we get zoo.

5.11 Anonymous

If, Cypris, you watch over those at sea,
Preserve me also: though I am ashore,
My ship is sinking and I look to drown.

5.16 Marcus Argentarius

Moon with your horns of gold, and shining stars
That Ocean welcomes into his embrace,
Come shed your light and be my witnesses:
For Ariste, whose very breath is myrrh,
Has gone away and has abandoned me.
A week has passed and still I cannot find
Her who ensorcelled me; and yet I swear
That I shall trap her, running her to ground
With aid of Aphrodite's silver hounds.

Two wet poems of pining. Aphrodite was the Greek goddess of sex and procreation, part of a line of goddesses stretching back through Phoenician Astarte and Semitic Ishtar to Innana of the Sumerians, the first literate civilization of the ancient Near East, and continuing into the Roman Venus. Her name is probably pre-Greek, though the Greeks loved to construct etymologies and the epic poet Hesiod (**5.113**) explained it with reference to the foam of the sea, **aphros**. She had many titles, and poets often address her as the Paphian, Cyprian/Cypris, or Cytherean/Cytherea in reference to her great cult centres at Paphos on Cyprus and at Kythera. Both islands claimed to be her birthplace, proposing separate origin stories. She was a flexible goddess with broad interests, honoured everywhere for fertility and sexual pleasure but by Spartans as a warrior. Worshippers might call on her as Aphrodite **Ouranios** or **Pandēmos**, a goddess of the heavens or of the whole (**pan**) people (**dēmos**). Plato's account of the Heavenly Aphrodite in his *Symposium* (**5.65**) encouraged classically educated members of late nineteenth-century Britain's emergent homosexual subculture to embrace the label 'Uranian', a backward-looking first step on the road to a new concept of sexual identity in which we all now participate.

Aphrodite had more than one genealogy (look, an *-ology*!, **5.10**) but Hesiod's account of her name had her born from the foam that rose when Zeus, chief god of the up-and-coming Olympians, castrated his father Kronos (leader of the old firm, called Titans) and flung his severed genitals into the sea. She was ever after associated with islands and seafarers. Sailors prayed to Aphrodite of Fair Voyage (**Euploios**) before any journey. The anonymous poet of 5.11 presents himself as a mariner in peril on the seas of love in the hope that Aphrodite will combine her roles and rescue him from disaster by bending the heart of the boy or girl with whom he is besotted.

Marcus Argentarius, a poet with a Roman name (**5.32**), keeps a restless vigil that echoes Sappho's (fr. 16B) from the earliest recorded days of choral song: 'The moon has set, and the Pleiades; it is the middle of the night, the hours go by, and I lie down alone.' The moon and stars stand in for a lamp (**5.7**) as his source of light and his witnesses. The girl he misses is literally Best—her name is the feminine form of **aristos**, the superlative form of the adjective **agathos** (good). **Aristos** does not look very much like **agathos**: Greek is on the whole a well-behaved language but some of the commonest verbs and adjectives get broken in use, just like in English (nobody says good–gooder–goodest, I goed, or I haved). On a vocabulary note, aristocracy puts power (**krateia**) in the hands of the best people, self-chosen; democracy gives power to the **dēmos**, the whole citizen body of the **polis**. A populist who seeks to manipulate that citizen body is a demagogue.

The 'I' of Marcus' poem feels he has been bewitched. Ancient authors were fascinated with the figure of the worker of spells; such characters in literature are invariably women, whose magical rites often invoke the female-gendered moon as their helper and co-conspirator, but the material evidence for magicians in real life points in the opposite direction. To judge by examples found on papyri and *ostraka* (potsherds), ancient erotic spells were invariably commissioned by men seeking to control women who were not interested in them. Marcus instead puts his trust in the persuasive power of cash, as does Antipater in the poem that follows.

In the second century AD the satirical essayist Lucian of Samosata (**10.30**) imagined the moon as a world with its own inhabitants, one that humans might conceivably visit. His *True History* inspired the fantastic voyages of (among others) Jonathan Swift, Jules Verne, and H. G. Wells, making him the accidental ancient prototype of modern science fiction.

5.30 Antipater of Thessalonica

The every utterance of Maeon's son
Was splendid, but he hit the utmost peak
When he picked Aphrodite's epithet:
'The golden.' For you see, if you bear coin,

You are a friend—no porter in your way,
No dog chained at the door. But if you come
Unminted, then the dog is Cerberus.
O grasping principles of capital!
What injuries you wreak on poverty.

'Maeon's son' translates **Maeonides**, a traditional name for Homer (7.2), whose epics assign descriptive epithets to their various heroes and divinities, one or two words long. Achilles for instance is very often 'swift-footed' (**podas ōkus**) no matter what he is doing—and for most of the *Iliad* he sits around and lets everyone else do the work; the Trojan leader in battle is 'brilliant' (**phaidimos**) Hector 'of the shining helmet' (**koruthaiolos**); the Greek chief Agamemnon is 'lord of men' (**anax andrōn**). The word for these is *epithets*.

The metre of ancient epic is *hexameter*, a line consisting of six metrical units called *feet*, each of them either a *dactyl* (dum-di-di) or *spondee* (dum-dum). That's easier than you'd think to remember because if you say 'dactyl and spondee' you've just said a *dactyl* and a *spondee*. Strictly speaking ancient metre is about syllable length, not emphasis. Here is the first line of the *Iliad*, first in Greek ad then transcribed with the long vowels marked and the divisions between feet marked with a vertical line:

μῆνιν ἄειδε θεὰ Πηληϊάδεω Ἀχιλῆος
Mē-nin a-|ei-de the-|ā Pē-|lēi-a-de | ō Akh-il-|ē-os
Dum-di-di | dum-di-di | dum-dum | dum-di-di | dum-di-di | dum-dum.

Strictly speaking that last foot goes dum-di and is called an *anceps*—lines aways end dactyl-and-spondee and the final syllable of that last spondee is allowed to be either long or short—

but you get the idea. When there are more lots more dactyls than spondees, which is basically always, you'll also see it called *dactylic hexameter*. You might hear horror stories about a thing called *elision* but that's something you only need to worry about in Latin poetry, which imports Greek metres (so sophisticated!) but is rubbish at fitting into them because hey, wrong language. Homeric name-plus-epithet combinations evolved within an originally oral poetic tradition to fit this metre neatly (they very often sit at the end of the line) while still getting to the heart of who these characters are.

There are two Antipaters in the Greek Anthology. The first came from Sidon in what is now the Lebanon, and wrote in the second century BC; this is the second, from Macedonia. This witty and versatile poet came to Rome around 30 BC and caught the attention of powerful aristocrats, including the politician Lucius Calpurnius Piso and, most importantly, Augustus, who was just then becoming established as Emperor under the modest-sounding title of *Princeps* (First Citizen). Over the next several decades Antipater did well out of celebrating the achievements of Rome's new first family and its friends. There are poems for instance on the foundation of Nicopolis, the 'Victory City' established by Augustus near the site of his victory over Antony and Cleopatra at Actium (9.553), and to accompany the gift to Piso of a sturdy hat to keep him snug on campaign (6.335). But he wrote love poems and epitaphs too, and sympathized with the victims of historic Roman aggression (7.493).

This is a poem about getting in to see a girl without her family finding out. Bribes are the trick, says Antipater. This is something Ovid might have written, and hardly calculated to appeal to Augustus, who legislated for family values and took seriously his position as Rome's highest-ranking priest. He was *Pontifex Maximus*, literally bridge-builder-in-chief, a title that remains in use: Popes are still Pontiffs. Readers in Italy and elsewhere may well have pictured the house of Antipater's poem with its porter's cubbyhole and guard-dog as a typical Roman *domus*, its door open in daytime to display the family's wealth and good taste but barred at night and always watched by a doorman. Several houses excavated at Pompeii have frescoes just inside the threshold with the slogan *CAVE CANEM*, 'beware of the dog', accompanied by pictures of a fierce-looking dog on a lead.

5.32 MARCUS ARGENTARIUS

Melissa is your name, 'the Honey-bee'.
All that your flower-fond namesake can achieve,
You achieve also. Woman, this I know,
And take to heart. Your kisses are so sweet
That honey even trickles from your lips;
And when you ask for payment, I am stung;
You jab me with your venom, cruelly.

Ancient readers will immediately have taken Melissa to be the working name of a **hetaira** (see **5.138**). In a slightly later period we meet a slew of such names in Lucian's sitcom, *Dialogues of Courtesans*, where another Melissa rubs shoulders with girls such as Chrysis (Goldie), Leaina (Lioness), Pannychis (All-Nighter), and Glycera (Sweetie), as well as escorts bearing the names of the legendary courtesans of old, Laïs and Thaïs.

Melissa means bee, or sometimes honey, and the poem builds on the inseparability of the two. Marcus gets the honeyed kisses he had been hoping for, but is stung by the bill afterwards. This part of Book 5 of the Anthology concentrates on how galling it is for a man to have to pay for sexual pleasure; for instance, Cillactor AP 5.29:

> Fucking is sweet. Who says it isn't? Still,
> Any and every time it asks for coin,
> Fucking is bitterer than hellebore.

We know nothing about Marcus Argentarius except that he wrote in the early Roman Empire, probably the first half of the first century AD. His transmitted epithet *argentarius* suggests a background in finance. The word is Latin, and the first name 'Marcus' also strongly suggests Roman credentials, but he was probably not Roman by language and culture: all his attested work is in Greek. By the first century plenty of Greeks had acquired Roman citizenship in one way or another; the satirical epigrammatist Lucillius, a likely contemporary of Marcus who was the main model for the Latin epigrams of Martial, bears the slightly mistransliterated name of a famous Roman *gens* and was active in Rome under Nero. In any case Marcus is an extraordinarily common Roman first name (*praenomen*), shared with Martial and countless others.

Honey was indispensable. It was the ancient world's culinary sweetener and was also used as a preservative as well as in many medical and cosmetic recipes. The body of Alexander the Great was said to have been preserved in honey after his death, as (wrote Herodotus) had those of ancient Syrians long before. For culinary use, those in the know favoured the mountain thyme honeys of Hymettus in Attica and Hybla in Sicily. Bee husbandry is the main focus of the fourth and concluding book of the *Georgics*, Virgil's didactic epic on the dignity of farming and estate management. He describes his hard-working bees as *parvos Quirites*, 'little Romans', a miniature civilization with much to teach us about our own—including the natural inevitability of periods of civil war such as those from which his Rome had only recently emerged under the new leadership of Augustus (**5.30**). Virgil tells you how to replace a lost swarm by killing an ox and letting it rot, an ancient method called by the Greeks **bougonia** (ox-generation) and with a biblical variant that you can still see illustrated on Tate and Lyle's tins of syrup and treacle ('out of strength, sweetness'). The sources swear to its efficacy.

5.33 Parmenion

Lord of Olympus, as a rain of gold
You visited Danäe, that the girl
Might be persuaded to it by a gift,
Not yield in terror before Kronos' son.

5.34 The Same

Zeus had Danäe in exchange for gold,
And I have you for gold: I cannot dare
To spend more liberally than did He.

Two further poems on the same theme as 5.32. We know nothing about their author, who shares his name with one of Alexander the Great's most trusted generals. Ancient history fans may have met that general as *Parmenio*; both forms are fine. The one with

-ōn is a transliteration of the Greek; the other is its Latinized form. Latin language has always been the bedrock of studying classics in the West, with Greek coming in from the Renaissance as an add-on for abler students at the prestigious seats of learning; and ancient Latin authors wrote about the Greeks a lot, so our long collective conversations about them often use the names by which Romans knew them. **Thoukudidēs** becomes Thucydides, **Aiskhulos**, Aeschylus, **Platōn**, Plato, and so on. The Greeks wrote 'k'; the Romans, 'c', for the same sound, and there's still no 'k' in modern Italian. The letter 'y' is still called *ygrec* in French because Romans used it specifically to represent the Greek 'u' (called upsilon). They had their own letter 'u/v' but it was too busy to take on extra jobs.

So partly the Romans tweaked Greek names because they used a slightly changed alphabet, which with a couple of further changes ('j', 'w') became the one we use today; but partly also because both languages are *inflected*. What this means is that nouns, verbs, and such—including the Greek word for 'the' (**6.254**)—change their endings depending on what jobs they are doing in the sentence. They fall into families called 'declensions' (nouns/pronouns/adjectives) and 'conjugations' (verbs), each of which has its own set of endings for those various jobs. When Romans met a Greek personal name ending in **-ōn** they treated them as if they were good old Latin names like Cato, lopping off the **-n** and taking it from there.

Parmenio(n)'s two poems work well as a pair. The myth of Danae is one of many in which Zeus resorts to tricks so he can sleep with mortal women without his wife Hera finding out (she usually does). Since Zeus is king of the gods, the poet only needs this one mythical exemplar to justify his own actions; if there were more, the poem would be a *priamel*.

5.44 Rufinus

The *Satisfaction* and her sister-ship,
The *Bachelor's Delight*, are courtesans;
Their home port, Samos. All of you young men,
Steer clear of Aphrodite's piracy:
He that they grapple onto will go down,
And taste the briny of this harbour town.

Port towns have always been good at separating sailors from their pay, and busy Samos in the early centuries AD can have been no exception. What's more, piracy was a real problem in the ancient world—Julius Caesar's civil war opponent Pompey had made his name suppressing it. But that is by the by; this poem is included to make a point about translators and why you should never quite trust us.

Here is a version a century old, by Frederick Adam Wright:

The Frenchy and the Privateer
Each night you'll see upon the pier,
Or else patrolling in the town,
Gulping poor silly youngsters down.
Beware these pirate-craft, my friends—
Such skirmishes have bitter ends.

Rhyming is good (small poems like to rhyme), but also bad (the meaning gets bent to fit the form). The rhyme at the end of my own poem reworks one of Wright's (a nod to tradition), but must pad to round it out ('of this harbour town' is harmless but has no basis in the Greek). This kind of thing happens all the time.

But what to do with the names of the ships? In the Greek they are the *Lembion* and *Kerkourion*. The **lembos** and **kerkouros** were two types of small, fast warship that must have been grand for

29

sneaky forays from hidden coves. In grammatical terms, **lembion** and **kerkourion** are their diminutive forms ('little boat'), which in Greek can suggest affection or humour ('Boaty'). But knowing this does not much help a translator who wants to figure out the point and get *a version of it* across. In a bygone age of wooden ships and iron men the sailor's terms of art bled into everyday English, but most of us now have no clue that 'by and large' and 'the bitter end' were ever nautical at all, still less what they once meant. (Long shot, toe the line, taken aback . . . the list goes on.)

Wright addressed the problem by choosing types of seaborne threat from a bygone but still culturally resonant age of naval warfare—a good choice, I think. My own version lifts names of actual pirate ships from a website called 'allthingsboat'. *Satisfaction* was Henry Morgan's, he of the spiced rum; *Bachelor's Delight*, William Dampier's. In an early version I even had the young men of Samos 'walk the plank and drown', to rhyme with 'down', but I decided that was a yo-ho-ho too far. As it is, my name choices added a sexual frisson that was probably not there for Rufinus' own readers. Some things are always lost in translation, but others can be found, too.

The last couplet warns potential customers that their experience will be traumatic. Ancient patriarchy posited that performing oral sex was a passive act and therefore degrading to an adult male citizen. Do not look to antiquity for a good time in bed.

5.44 Cillactor

A young girl ripe for marriage makes best show
Of her small assets, not by any art,
But by acquainting buyers with her part.

5.63 Marcus Argentarius

I used to think you were from Sicily,
Antigone; you are 'Aetolian' now,
And look at me: I have become a 'Mede'.

Two poems about male entitlement, but that is Book 5 of the Anthology for you. Nothing is known for sure about Cillactor, whom some scholars would like to identify with another, equally minor Anthology poet called Callicter, really just to make all our lives simpler.

The Antigone of Marcus' poem shares her name with the daughter of Oedipus about whom Sophocles wrote one of his best-known tragedies. Antigone means something like 'Born to oppose'. Lots of Greek personal names mean things: Horse-lover (Philippus), Fine in the fighting (Callimachus), Famed for wisdom (Sophocles), Ruling many (Poycrates), Gift of Artemis (Artemidorus). People enjoyed arguing about what Homer's name might mean: a rare word for 'hostage', or maybe 'the thigh' (**ho mēros**)? But then they enjoyed arguing about anything and everything to do with Homer, because his *Iliad* and *Odyssey* were so basic to their sense of who they were, and endlessly good to play around with.

Aetolia is a mountainous region of central Greece, bordering Epirus and Thessaly to the north, but Marcus is not seriously suggesting that Antigone (who probably only exists for the purposes of this poem) is from there. Nor has he actually become a 'Mede', which means more or less the same as Persian. The main reason this epigram is here is to illustrate the impossibility of faithful translation—some might say always, but certainly and much more so when the original language is being used in a slippery way. Figures of speech are one example, because they are so metaphorical: you could translate 'it's as broad as it's long' or 'by and large' (5.44) into French or Japanese with exact lexical accuracy and leave your audience baffled. Obscenities are tricky for much the same reason, especially sexual ones, because different cultures have different maps of how sex works and how it might tell on a person.

Jokes are notoriously hard to bring across into another language. People only laugh because they 'get' the things left unsaid, and those depend on situational common knowledge as well as linguistic fluency. A translator of (say) Aristophanes can update the jokes and make people laugh, translate word-for-word and have the jokes make no sense, or try to strike some kind of balance: there is no one right answer. All 'fidelity' can mean is a person's least bad compromise on the day.

Puns and plays on words are an even harder challenge, and that is what we have here. Antigone is 'Aetolian' because she is 'asking' (Greek verb **aiteō**) to be paid (compare 5.32). Marcus or the protagonist of the poem (you can decide the distinction for yourself) is a 'Mede' (**Mēdos**) because he is not (Greek **mē**) going to pay (Greek verb **didōmi**, of which **dōs** is a participle form). This is Paton's explanation, and he was right. The old Loeb of the Anthology is a serious resource; you should grab it (**Introduction, p. 9**).

5.64 Asclepiades

Fall, snow and hail, and turn the heavens dark;
Flash, lightning, and pour out your churning cloud

Across the planet. If you strike me down,
Then and then only shall I quit my way;
But if you leave me standing, I shall go
And revel in my night-time serenade,
For I have dodged far worse. Stronger than you
The god who now compels me on my way,
And once, o Zeus, you did his bidding too,
Descending to a chamber made of brass
And seeking entrance as a shower of gold.

The name Asclepiades literally means 'son of Asclepius', the heroic and half-divine patron of Greek medicine, whose own mythical sons Machaōn and Podalirius famously served as combat medics to the Greek army that besieged Troy. Born early in the fourth century, Asclepiades was one of the very first poets to write and perform epigram as literary poetry rather than for inscription. He came to Alexandria from wealthy and well-connected Samos (**5.44**), which was becoming an important Ptolemaic naval base.

The myth in the closing lines is again that of Danae, imprisoned by her father King Acrisius of Argos in a metal vault (or in some versions a tower) after an oracle warned that any son she bore would kill him. Zeus got in anyway, and Danae's son by him did eventually kill her father, by blameless accident. The son was Perseus, hero of *Clash of the Titans*.

In this poem a bedraggled would-be lover marches across town to the door of the woman he fancies, probably with some friends in tow despite the foul weather. The hour is late: they have come from a symposium (**5.81**), so everyone has had a few drinks; they sing as they make their way through the darkened streets (**5.7**). If, as seems likely, the protagonist finds the door bolted in his face

and nobody answers when he knocks, he will stay a while sere-
nading his girl before he hangs his garland of flowers on the door
and calls it a night. This ritual night-time procession was called
a **kōmos** and must have been a nuisance when people were try-
ing to get some sleep. The speaker is compelled by the god Erōs
(**5.10**), Desire, and he asks Zeus, god of thunder and wielder of
the lightning-bolt, to see him safe to his destination. Compare
the anonymous **5.168**:

> Hit me with fire, hit me with driving snow,
> Hit me with lightning even, if you like,
> Haul me to crags and to the open sea;
> For when a man succumbs to his desires
> And is subdued by Love, he can withstand
> Even the fire of Zeus' thunderbolt.

After all, the stories make it clear that Zeus is as susceptible to
human beauty as is any mortal—his infatuation with Ganymede
(**12.65**) is a case in point—so he ought to show sympathy for a fel-
low sufferer. If the kōmast makes it there alive, he will know that
the king of the gods is on his side, a good omen for how the even-
ing may end.

The shut-out lover (adopted by Roman elegists as the *exclusus
amator*, **5.164**) was one of Asclepiades' favourite themes. Compare
for instance 5.145, which really ought to be in Book 12, the Boyish
Muse, not here:

> You wreaths that hang beside the bifold door:
> Stay here a while, and do not be in haste
> To scatter petals moistened with my tears—
> For lovers' eyes are always showering.
> But when it opens and you see that boy,

34

Scatter this rain of mine upon his head,
That his blond hair may drink the tears I shed.

5.65 Anonymous

Zeus as an eagle came to Ganymede,
That godlike boy, and as a swan he came
To fair-haired Leda—Helen was her child;
And so, you see, the two are not the same.
Each is beyond compare. And of the twain
Each has its advocates and partisans;
My difference is to choose them equally.

A poem about what we would call bisexuality. The Greeks and Romans had no word for it, or for sexuality generally. Lexically and medically, homosexuality is an invention of the late nineteenth century. The writer who imported it to English from German sexology was the (in our terms) gay rights pioneer, John Addington Symonds. An excellent classical scholar, he deprecated it as an impure mix of Greek (**homos**, same) and Latin (*sexus*, the obvious). He would have loathed 'television' for the same pedantic reason. I am not deprecating pedants; the world needs them (us), and pedantry is fun.

Bisexuality is a newer word than homosexuality—but then, so is heterosexuality (from Greek **heteros**, meaning other). In lexical and medical terms straightness is an after-effect of gayness. In the 1970s and 1980s Michel Foucault, the heroic analyst of freedoms and constraints across documented human history, mapped out a model of ancient sexuality that centred not around stable same- or opposite-sex attractions or 'identities', a modern word with no ancient equivalent, but around control: the powerful (essentially, adult male citizens) used the less powerful (women, juveniles, the enslaved) for pleasure, while constantly keeping in view the risk of losing power by losing self-control and thereby becoming less manly. The citizen male love-poet's erotic conceit of becoming a slave to love (the Latin trope of *servitium amoris*, familiar from Ovid and such) is by this reckoning a holiday in somebody else's misery, playing at being powerless through the conceit that Erōs is now one's temporary master. The great difference Foucault saw between Greece and Rome was in the implications for citizen status when the boy became a man. To be wooed and eventually won by a socially suitable admirer was fine for a young Greek, but the same behaviour would bring permanent disgrace (*stuprum*) on his Roman equivalent.

Foucault was clearly basically right, and his work transformed Greek and Roman studies from the 1980s onwards, but some people in antiquity clearly always did have a sense of falling outside that pattern and indeed of possessing a stable sexual and romantic identity, of being in our sense straight or gay or bi. A famous example is the speech attributed to the comic playwright Aristophanes in Plato's *Symposium*, according to which we are all in search of the other half that will complete us: maybe male, maybe female, but when we find them we will know.

5.78 'Plato'

As I was kissing Agathon, my soul
Halted upon my lips; the wretched thing
Was on its way to transmigrate to him.

5.80 The Same

I am an apple, and a certain man
Threw me because he loves you. Just agree,
Xanthippe: for you soon decay, like me.

Each epigram in the Anthology comes with an explanatory head-ing, called a **lemma**. In some books it tells us the poem's subject (Books 1, 3, 8) or its metre (Book 13), but most of the time we get the name of the author believed to have written it. The headings are very useful, but sometimes they wobble; this is a case where the attribution must be wrong, so I have put it in scare-quotes.

Plato (fifth to fourth centuries BC) was Socrates' chief disciple and the author of many famous dialogues in which Socrates ques-tions and confounds his Athenian contemporaries. Typically these dialogues are named for their main interlocutors: *Crito*, *Gorgias*, *Meno*, and so on. They're not transcripts of real conversations; Socrates was dead by the time Plato started writing them. One might instead call them exercises in reputation management, Plato's and his mentor's alike. The unknown author(s) of the epigrams knew Socrates in exactly the same way we do, through Plato's dialogues and a couple of essays by Xenophon, and the characters in the poems are all from that pre-existing literature.

Agathon was a tragic playwright, and by all accounts irresistibly gorgeous. His plays are all lost and he is best known as one of the participants in Plato's *Symposium* (**5.65**), where like all the other guests he gives a speech in praise of love. His name in Greek ends in **-ōn** just like those of Plato (**Platōn**), Crito (**Kritōn**), and such, names that come to us through Latin (**5.34**); if Roman or mediaeval authors had been interested in him we would know him as *Agatho*. There is no great logic to these things. Xanthippe was Socrates'

37

wife and the mother of his sons; this poem conjures up their court-ship, a topic in which Plato had no interest whatsoever. An apple was a classic lover's gift, and the Socrates of this epigram is hoping for some premarital action: in the poem that comes between these two in the Anthology he begs her 'if you love me back, then make the catch, | And share with me your maiden innocence'. A young person's moment of peak physical beauty, their bloom (**anthos**), was fleeting, and a shrivelling apple or wilting rose was a reminder to get good use out of that bloom before it spoiled.

Socrates did not write these love poems (he wrote nothing), and nor did Plato, for the simple reason that literary epigram did not exist yet. In the fifth and fourth centuries BC, epigram's uses were strictly inscriptional. Plato was no more an erotic epigram-matist than Shakespeare was a novelist or Dickens a blogger. The Xanthippe and Agathon poems are ancient fanfiction, pure and simple. Their anonymous author is showing off his or her mas-tery of canon. Readers enjoyed imagining the epigrams were the real thing, and Meleager boasts in his preface of weaving into his *Garland* of poetry (**5.140**) the 'golden bough' of a Plato whom he calls 'forever godlike' on account of his timeless wisdom.

5.81 Dionysius the Sophist

> You with the roses: rosy is your charm.
> What do you have for sale, though? Is it you?
> The roses? Or a package of the two?

The after-dinner party called the *symposium* (the Latinized form of **sumposion**, literally drinking together) was where Greek male citizens set aside the day's cares and socialized. In the archaic period it had been strictly aristocratic—you can get a sense of what it was like from surviving lyric poetry, translated by Martin West for the World's Classics—but in the classical and Hellenistic periods it attracted a broader social mix. It was still a formal occasion with etiquette around the mixing and distribution of wine (Greeks had a horror of letting drink get the better of them). There was always music, guests were expected to contribute to the entertainment (a song perhaps), and everyone wore plaited wreaths of flowers on their heads, so as to be pretty and smell nice. At the end of the evening, a lovestruck partygoer might detour on the way home to hang his wreath at the door of his intended (**5.64**). Garlands wilted quickly, and flower-sellers did a brisk trade.

The addressee of this poem is definitely a girl or woman (the Greek makes that clear) but roses were strongly associated with pretty boys, as in this poem by Strato of Sardis, a poet who specialized in pederastic verse (12.8):

> Passing just now the garland-seller's place,
> I saw a lad who wove a clustered wreath;
> Nor did I pass unwounded. As I paused,
> I whispered to him, 'Is that wreath for sale?
> What will you take for it?' The young man's blush
> Was redder than his roses; he leaned in
> And said, 'Be off, in case my father sees'
> I bought some wreaths, maintaining the pretence,
> And back at home I garlanded the gods,
> Praying to them the boy might soon be mine.

Or this one, by an unknown poet (**5.142**):

> Say, is the garland Dionysius' rose,
> His bloom of loveliness, or is that boy

39

Himself the rose that makes the garland shine?
It seems to me the crown that falls behind.

So flowers in the Anthology tradition stand for at least three things: the symposium, youthful beauty, and the work of anthologization itself. The Greek for flower, **anthos**, survives in garden plant names such as chrysanthemum (plant with golden flowers). To 'anthologize' is literally to gather flowers, as would a flower-seller for weaving a wreath; indeed the two first great prototypes of the Anthology, by Meleager (first century BC) and Philip (first century AD), took the title *Garland* (**Stephanos**)—and yes, that is where the name Stephen comes from. Meleager opened his *Steve* with an elaborate verse preface that compared each chosen poet to a type of flowering plant, woven all together into a figurative wreath far bigger (and spikier) than could possibly be worn for real.

More widely, roses were considered the epitome of delicate beauty. Old Comedy preserves some colloquial usages: 'You have spoken roses of me' (Aristophanes); 'a pig among roses' (Crates), the latter the equivalent of our 'bull in a china shop'. A confession: I did not know until recently that epitome is four syllables, to rhyme with Penelope and catastrophe and other Greek-derived polysyllables. For years I rhymed it with 'home' and 'tome' and, in my defence, 'palindrome' (**9.457**).

5.85 Asclepiades

You hoard your maidenhead, and to what gain?
When you go down to Hades, bashful girl,
You will not find yourself a lover there;
The pleasures of the Cyprian are meant

For us, the living, who as bones and dust
Will sleep forever on the Acheron.

5.87 Rufinus

Melissias denies she is in love,
And yet her body shrieks the quiverful
Of arrows that have pierced it. So her step
Is frantic, like the racing of her breath;
Hollow the eyes where love-darts found their mark.
But, unfulfilled Desires, I call on you
By Cythereia of the shining crown:
This woman who disdains your mother's fame—
Burn her till she admits, 'I feel your flame'.

Two poems on reluctant young women; epigram's would-be
lover-boys cannot imagine what puts them off (**5.64**). Again we
see Aphrodite addressed by her cult titles Cypris and Cytherea
(**5.16**). Cypress trees have nothing to do with Cyprus—they are
named for Cyparissus, a beautiful boy after whom Apollo lusted
with the usual life-limiting implications (Ovid tells his story in
Metamorphoses Book 10)—but copper does; the Romans knew it
as Cyprian bronze (*aes cyprium*), which later corrupted to *cuprum*
and ended up in the periodic table as Cu.

   The Acheron is one of the five rivers of Hades, the most famous
of the rest being the Styx (**7.69**), river of hatred and disgust; there
were rivers too of lamentation (Cocytus), forgetfulness (Lethe),
and fire (Phlegethon). The Acheron is the river of painful griev-
ing. It is also the name of a real river in north-western Greece,
much in the way that Olympus is the home of the gods in the sky
but also a real mountain in north-eastern Greece that one might

potentially climb; not that the Greeks were ever much interested in climbing mountains. This last fact was later to bother the Victorians (**5.16**) who—it's a long story—had decided that the British were the new ancient Greeks, but who were also invested in a decidedly un-classical concept of natural grandeur in high places (the Romantic Sublime). Yes, we digress, but why else would we be sharing this time together?

Melissias is named for honey, of course (**5.32**). She denied the power of Erōs until she became his target; now she shows physical symptoms of lovesickness that recall Sappho and the Hellenistic poets (**5.10**). Her name takes an Ionian Greek form. The two main dialects of Greek were Attic and Ionic, named for but not exclusive to Attica (of which the principal **polis** or city-state was Athens) and Ionia (in our terms the western coast of Turkey) respectively. There were a number of differences but the easiest one to spot is that where Attic puts **-tt-**, Ionic has **-ss-**. If she was Athenian, Melissias would be Melittias. The Ionians looked out over the sea and called it **thalassa**, but when Attic Xenophon and his fellow mercenaries made it back to the same coast from their march into the Persian interior (a tale remembered with advantages is his own *Anabasis*) they shouted **thalatta, thalatta** in their sheer relief at being back in sight of their natural environment.

Over time, a simplified form of Ionian Greek won out and became the **koinē**, literally the common tongue of the whole eastern Mediterranean and territories adjacent. The universality of this language facilitated the spread of the jumble of epistles and subliterary mystery-texts that in winnowed form we call the New Testament.

The name of the Acheron derives from a Greek word for suffering, **akhos**, that looks very like the English 'ache'. They are not etymologically connected, but Samuel Johnson was sure they were, so his *Dictionary of the English Language* (1755) changed the word's spelling from the previously standard 'atche' (rhymes with hatch) to bring your niggling pains into line with those of the ancient Greeks.

5.93 Rufinus

I have put on my armour against Love,
A breastplate made of reasoned argument.
He will not beat me if he comes alone,
In single combat—I shall hold my own,
Mortal against immortal. Then again,
If he should team with Bacchus, what to do?
Alone, I shall be helpless against two.

There were various 'reasoned arguments' around love and sex in the ancient world. The first Greek philosophers (the Presocratics, so called by us simply because they came before Socrates) concerned themselves first and foremost with the nature of reality. What was the world made of—water and air, or fire, or maybe numbers? Then came philosophical schools that extrapolated ethics out of physics. What was life for and what might it mean to live it well, in the world such as they variously believed it to be?

In a cosmos of atoms and void (7.56) with no supreme being or organizing principle beyond the tendency of systems to run down, it was obvious to Epicureans that the only sensible goal in life was to have a nice time. They were hedonists, from the Greek word for pleasure (**hēdonē**), but their hedonism was rational: to maximize pleasure a person had to work on minimizing physical and mental pain, and prioritize pleasures that were materially and psychologically sustainable. Sex was a natural appetite and good fun for men and women alike, but mixing it with love was likely to result in heartbreak. Go with 'some Venus of the street', says Lucretius (4.1058) in his Latin epic of the way things are (*De Rerum Natura*), and have a straightforwardly transactional good time. In our current terms he professed aromanticism. Antipater of Thessalonica (5.109) backs up his point that it is silly to make work for yourself in the pursuit of having fun:

> Europa is a nice Athenian girl,
> And you can have her for a silver coin,
> Need fear no interruption, nor expect
> That she will quibble. And her bed is clean,
> Quite spotless, and she keeps a warming fire
> If it is chilly out. When you became
> A bull, friend Zeus, your labour was in vain.

Stoic physics (again **7.56**) was the complete opposite. Stoics inhabited a radically connected universe, permeated by divine spirit and running according to a definite and excellent plan. Accordingly their priority was to get with the plan and do their part. A necessary first stage was to achieve and maintain self-control—and that was easier said than done. Rationality was a difficult balancing act and indulging in any strong emotion, even a positive one, could easily upend it. Some Stoics consequently agreed with Lucretius about prostitutes, if about nothing else. Others thought the only legitimate purpose for sex was to make babies within marriage. Then as now, arguments about sex tended to lead the arguer to whatever position they had already emotionally staked out.

Stoic thinking about sex owed a good deal to the Cynics (**7.49**), who valued shamelessness (**anaideia**) and aimed to cut the bullshit from sexual and romantic relationships as from every other aspect of human life. Sex according to them ought not to be treated as special or mysterious. According to later sources the female Cynic philosopher Hipparchia was determined to marry the much older and physically ugly fellow-Cynic Crates, and they consummated their union with outdoor sex in full public view. Cynicism's founder, the barrel-dwelling Diogenes, masturbated openly in the marketplace (**agora**)—you could get agoraphobia just thinking about it.

5.105 Marcus Argentarius

Within the demi-monde, Mēnophila
Is said to have her own celestial sphere,
A whole alternate cosmos, since her tastes
Are polymorphous in perversity.
Chaldean seers, go study at her knee:
For her strange heavens can accommodate
The Twins and Dog-star simultaneously.

I include this epigram by a Roman-named poet as a lesson in the limits of what we understand when we make or use translations. I am very happy with my version but I am not quite sure what it means.

The 'demi-monde' of the first line is the plural of a rare poetic feminine form of a word that the dictionary defines as 'lewd, lustful'. It is used primarily to describe women; there is a separate word for slutty men (**6.254**). By transference it is metaphorical for wantonness and luxuriance, which by patriarchal logic are coded as feminine.

W. R. Paton, who translated the Greek Anthology for the Loeb Classical Library, saw two obscene double entendres in this poem that I cannot unsee. He was careful to veil them in Latin—what Edward Gibbon, author of *Decline and Fall of the Roman Empire*, once called 'the obscurity of a learned language' (a later mis-quoter turned it to 'decent obscurity'). Here is the translation he gave his readers:

> Alius Menophilae qui dictum inter reliqua scorta mundus (vel decennia), alius ubi omnem adhibet impudicitiam. At vos Chaldaei accedite ad hanc; caelum (vel palatum) enim eius et Canem et Geminos intus habet.

Is everything clear? Of course not, and that was the intention. Completeness is the whole point of the Loeb series, and Paton had agreed to translate the complete Anthology, but he had never said into *what*. He was not the only early Loeb translator to work around sexual content in ways that now seem ridiculous but that made compelling sense to them at the time, and presumably to their editors and the marketing department as well. If you think Paton is bad, try looking at Walter Ker's awful old Loeb of the Latin epigrams of Martial—any time he suspects his author is turning sexual or scatological (and it's Martial, so, a lot), he switches into Italian. And this is not just any Italian: it is eighteenth-century Italian, from a version made long ago in London by a fencing mas-ter, and ransacked in the meantime for the Bohn Classical Library (the late nineteenth-century predecessor of Penguin Classics and the World's Classics) to cover up much the same dirty bits. Other translators in the early days of the Loeb series deliberately misled their readers or left things out completely. Paton's sins are minor compared to that. I would also like to cut him some slack because he was a much better classical scholar than Ker was, or than I am. In the postwar era (when Penguin Classics were still expurgated) Loeb's series editor quietly replaced the Latin versions with plain English: the rest was grand, though archaic, and most of it carries on being reprinted to this day (in the case of Volume 1 with revisions by Michael Tueller).

What it turns out Paton reckoned, once you translate his translation and then de-vague what you have translated, is that the 'celestial sphere' or 'cosmos' at the poem's beginning is Menophila's vagina and the 'heavens' at the end are her mouth. The 'Twins' Castor and Pollux (**6.149**) are attested as ancient slang for testicles (not breasts as in contemporary American English), so it seems likely that 'Dog' was a colloquial term for penis. Paton was probably right: an epigram by Nicarchus (11.328), rich (if that is the word) in Homeric quotation, turns cosmology and cosmogony into sexual innuendo in a similar way. 'Figs' in ancient Greek is a euphemism for haemorrhoids, and it's pretty clear what kind of thunderbolt Cleobulus is wielding:

> Hermogenes, Cleobulus, and I
> Once went all-in on Aristodice.
> The share I drew was 'her grey sea to dwell'—
> We split her parts between us, do you see,
> And did not each enjoy all equally.
> Hermogenes got 'hateful, gusting hall':
> He drew the last, and down he went below,
> Into the darkness of the haunted shore,
> Where figs are tumbled in the noisy gale.
> Imagine Cleobulus as our Zeus,

Ascending to 'the heavens' high above,
Taking his share with thunderbolt in hand.
'The earth remained in common to us all',
For there we spread our mat and took our share.

Chaldea is Akkadia, an early Mesopotamian culture known through its cuneiform tablets. By the sixth century BC it was long gone, but it remained a name to conjure with in any discussion of astronomy, astrology, and fortune-telling well into the Roman Empire.

5.108 Crinagoras

Poor girl! With what first word shall I begin,
And with what word make end and say farewell?
'Poor girl' is apt in all calamity.
You lovely woman, you have gone away,
Just as you were arriving at the peaks
Of youthful beauty and of character.
Prōte they called you, 'First', a fitting name:
All other creatures came in second place,
Conceding you unrivalled in your grace.

Like **5.96** but even more so, this poem is in completely the wrong place. It belongs in Book 7, the Anthology's collection of epitaphs. Its original readers would have known straight off that Prōte's name means First, but my translation has to spell it out. The puzzling question in the first line ('with what first word . . . ?') is actually cueing up the revelation of her name in the opening hexameter line of the original's third and final couplet (my version runs a couple of lines longer). The root of Prōte's name carries over into English words such as protagonist, prototype, protoplasm, even proton and protein.

Prōte's death was tragic because it squandered her potential just as she was coming to her **anthos** or **hōra** ('hour'), her brief acme of youthful brilliance. The Greeks saw physical beauty as a form of personal excellence that mirrored and typically accompanied moral soundness and good social standing. The girl Crinagoras mourns was the total package.

Billy Joel sang that 'Only the good die young', but plenty of the Anthology's epitaphs tell us otherwise. Insofar as we can estimate ancient demographics (and documentary papyrus discoveries are a sketchy base of evidence) there was massive die-off from illness in infancy, childhood, young adulthood—really across the curve. Enlarged understanding of the inner workings of the body (**7.158**) did not mean so much in practice without a realistic theory of, and reliable treatments for, infection and disease. Look at the Graeco-Roman funerary portraits found attached to mummies from the Fayum in Egypt (**6.341**), drawn not so much from life as from recent death, and you will not see many old faces.

Crinagoras is one of those Greek poets who, like Antipater of Thessalonica (**5.30**), supported the new world order being hammered out by Augustus and his collaborators in the late first century BC. His verses marked the life milestones of Rome's new first family—birthdays, safe returns from trips abroad (6.161, 9.239). His association with them lasted decades: he was with Augustus on an expedition to Spain in 27 BC, getting an education in the wiles of Alpine bandits along the way (9.516), and in AD 9 he put the best possible face on the Varus disaster, in which the Roman-trained Cherusci prince Arminius annihilated three legions in the Teutoburg Forest and forever ended Roman geopolitical ambitions east of the Rhine (7.741 and **9.291**).

Crinagoras' other epitaphs include one for Cleopatra Selene (7.633), the daughter of Cleopatra and Marc Antony, leaders of the losing side in the last phase of the dreadful civil wars that wrote off Rome's Republic:

> Rising at eventide, the very Moon
> Made her light dim and veiled her grief in night,
> Seeing her pretty namesake set and sink
> Lifeless in Hades' dark. For she had shared
> With Selene the beauty of her light,
> And merged her passing with her own eclipse.

Named for the goddess of the moon, Selene was ten when her parents died; raised from then on in Augustus' sister's household in Rome, she became an important political asset and took a leading role in bringing stability and wealth to Roman North Africa as queen of Numidia, Mauretania, and finally Cyrenaica. She and her husband Juba were buried in the Royal Mausoleum of Mauretania, still an imposing edifice.

5.113 Marcus Argentarius

> You used to be in love, Sosicrates,
> When you were rich; but now that you are poor,
> You have no time for love. Hunger's the cure.
> Upon a time, Mēnophila would say
> You were her 'sugar-daddy' and her 'bae',
> Who now pretends she has to ask your name:
> 'What man are you, from where, and of what town?'

It has been long in coming, but you grasped
The meaning of the adage in the end:
The man with nothing is nobody's friend.

If their poetry is any guide, poverty was a constant terror to Greeks of the archaic and early classical periods. There was no welfare state, and one bad harvest or lost cargo could mean disaster. The whole point of Hesiod's *Works and Days* is how not to starve to death, in a world in which people sometimes did just that. Fear of falling into destitution haunts the lyric poetry that preceded epigram as sympotic entertainment. Here are examples from Archilochus, Semonides, and Mimnermus (seventh century BC):

A man goes wandering, short of bread, out of his mind with fright . . .

. . . some
Die out at sea, by tempests buffeted
And the salt purple deep's unending waves,
When they can make no living from the land;
Others again fasten themselves a noose
And leave the sunlight by their own grim choice.

All kinds of worry come. One man's estate
Is falling, and there's painful poverty;
Another has no sons. . . .

Beginning in the Hellenistic age, pastoral poetry romanticized peasant life, with epigram playing an important role in the gentrification of collective memory for the privileged minority who were reading, not ploughing. Still the pessimism of Hesiod and the archaic lyric poets lived on.

The other thing that dissuaded potential romantic partners was old age. Philosophical weirdoes aside (**5.93**) there was no way a pretty young man or woman would go with someone ugly, and the signs of aging were considered ugly. For Mimnermus the joys of young love and the horrors of old age were inseparable (the translation is again Martin West's):

> What's life, what's joy, without love's heavenly gold?
> I hope I die when I no longer care
> For secret closeness, tender favours, bed,
> Which are the rapturous flowers that grace youth's prime
> For men and women. But when painful age
> Comes on, that makes a man loathsome and vile,
> Malignant troubles ever vex his heart;
> He is abhorred by boys, by women scorned. . . .

5.119 Crinagoras

> Turn on your left side, turn upon your right,
> Upon your empty bed, Crinagoras;
> But if Gemella lies not by your side,
> That lovely girl, then know the night will pass
> Not in sweet sleep, but weary suffering.

5.120 Philodemus

> Midnight had come, and so I stole away,
> Leaving my sleeping husband unaware,
> And never mind the rain that soaked me through;
> And did I come so we might sit and spoil
> Our time on trifles, not to speak our share
> And lie together as true lovers do?

Two Greek poets in Rome's world. We have met the Augustan court poet Crinagoras already (**5.108**); here we find him missing the intimate company of a young Roman woman whose name is Latin for Twin. Perhaps she has a sister. Philodemus meanwhile puts us into the point of view of just such a young woman, arriving at just such a clandestine encounter and starting to wonder why she risked coming all that way (**5.7**).

The long reign of Rome's first and most wearyingly moralistic emperor also saw the brief but brilliant flowering of Latin erotic elegy with Propertius, Tibullus, and Ovid, the last of whom ended up exiled for life to the Black Sea for what he later evasively described as 'a song and a screwup' (*carmen et error, Tristia* 2.207), inspiring many theories and fictions as to which poem and what kind of mistake. There was a woman erotic elegist as well, Sulpicia. Like Catullus before them, these poets drew on Hellenistic models to develop a sexy poetic universe that was squarely at odds with traditional local values. We will never know the full range of the texts on which they drew, some of which may be so completely lost that they fall into the category of unknown unknowns, but erotic epigram with its rich repertoire of tropes and motifs was a crucial ingredient in the mix.

We know as well that a whole slew of now lost Greek micro-epic (*epyllion*) was strip-mined as material on behalf of Cornelius Gallus, the famous first exponent of Roman erotic elegy, by a highly educated prisoner of war called Parthenius—the text of his *Erōtika Pathēmata* survives. Loosely translated, that title means 'the bad stuff that happens when people/gods get horny'. Gallus' own elegies are almost entirely lost, though, and it is hard to spot concrete signs of his successors using Parthenius as a resource (for a mean literary epitaph on him, see **13.71**). In any case the Roman poets must have had ideas of their own: their motif of love as a form of enslavement (*servitium amoris*) is not yet fully developed in the Anthology as we have it, and the idea of love as a form of legionary-style military service (*militia amoris*) was all their own.

Many of Philodemus' witty and sexy poems must have been composed on the Bay of Naples where he lived in fine style as the house intellectual of the rich and politically important Piso family (**5.30**) at Herculaneum. This was nearly a century before the local mountain went bang and buried the local towns under tons of ash and boiling slurry (AD 79). Vesuvius took everyone by surprise. Previously its mineral-rich soil had been great for vines, as again it is today, for now, thanks to that banging habit.

Philodemus curated extensive Greek and Latin libraries at the family mansion and wrote scathing philosophical and literary-critical tracts, flambéed parts of which were long ago unearthed at the site and are now being deciphered. The excavated villa itself became the model for the Getty Villa at Malibu. He was an Epicurean (**7.56**), a philosophy that marries well with seeking pleasure providing you do not let it take over your life. Here is another by him (5.107):

> 'You are a lovely creature, but I know
> To pay back friends with friendship in return,
> And bite the biter. I am fond of you,
> But do not give me grief, or rouse to rage
> The Muses in their stubborn cruelty.'
> Time and again I warned you, loud and clear,
> But you took in my words without a trace,
> Like the Ionian Sea. So now you cry
> And wail in endless sorrow, while I lie
> Within the bosom of a river-nymph.

5.122 Diodorus

Please don't, not even if he seems to you
More precious than your eyes, you budding son
Of famed Megistocles; nor if he gleams
Fresh-bathed by Graces; do not make that boy
The centre of your wild imaginings.
Yes, he is handsome, but he is not kind,
He is not innocent, instead is known
To many lovers, nor is he unschooled
In giving satisfaction. Be afraid:
Young sir, take care you do not fan the flame.

This poem by an author whose name (a very common one) means 'God's gift' is one of several in Book 5 that obviously were put here by mistake. They ought to be in Book 12, transmitted in the manuscript as the *Mousa Paidikē* or Boyish Muse. That title in turn does not exactly belong to the book that now wears it: rather, it belonged to a book by one gay poet, Strato of Sardis, or **Stratōn** in the original Greek (**5.34**), around which armature the anthologist Cephalas assembled the rest of the contents of Book 12 eight hundred or so years later. I myself would place him alongside Martial in the Rome of the later first century AD under Domitian; he is often dated to the reign of Hadrian in the early second century because he writes (in our terms) gay poetry and Hadrian was (in our terms) at least bi, but that's a thin argument and just a tad homophobic.

It goes both ways: there are a few poems in Book 12 that ought to be in Book 5, too. The Greek Anthology was a huge project and was probably not the only thing on Cephalas' mind. Also, some personal names were ambiguous. Here is where it gets confusing, all the more so in translation. Greek men whom we know under names ending in -ō (Plato, for instance) were **-ōn** in the original (**Platōn**) (**5.34**). Knowing this helps us tell them apart from Greek women's names, some of which *did* end -ō—Sappho, for instance. No Greek reader would have looked at the name 'Sappho' and thought for a moment that it might refer to a man. *But* there were also Greek women whose names ended **-iōn** because their names were diminutive forms; **Myrtiōn**, for instance, 'Lil' Myrtle'. *And* some men's personal names ended in that same diminutive form **-iōn** as well, so we have to factor in context. Here is a poem by Meleager from earlier in the book (**5.96**), filed in the Anthology as heterosexual but probably in the wrong place:

> Your kiss is birdlime, and your eyes are fire:
> No sooner do you look upon a man,
> Timarion, than he bursts into flames;
> And if you touch him, he is bound in chains.

There is another Timariōn poem in Book 5 (compare 5.204), but Cephalas placed a third one in Book 12 of the Anthology (12.109). In that case he took Timariōn to be a boy and I think that time he got it right. Names ending **-iōn** could go either way and I have sympathy for Cephalas' problems in sorting through them. He had a lot on his plate, and the ancient culture of romancing boys was alien to his own experience in Christian Byzantium a thousand years or so down the line.

5.125 Bassus

> I do not think that I shall ever fall
> As golden shower: let another one

Become an ox, or else a dulcet swan
Upon the riverbank. It is for Zeus
To keep these childish pastimes as his own.
For my part, I shall take my two brass coins
And pay them to Corinna as her fee,
And have no need for wings to carry me.

5.126 Philodemus

Our Mister A pays out his bodyweight,
Five talents' worth of silver for one go
With his Miss B, and shivers as he fucks,
And she is not good-looking anyway;
While I pay Lysianassa five brass coins
To fuck a dozen times, and, what is more,
She does it better and I do not care
Who knows about it. So I say to you:
Either I have gone crazy, or next time
She ought to take a hatchet to his balls.

Bassus and Philodemus run the numbers. His Epicurean beliefs
(**5.93**) give Philodemus an extra incentive not to overcommit: his
philosophy aims at simple and sustainable pleasures that will
not complicate his life or limit his options. He calls both 'Mister
A' and 'Miss B' by the Greek word **deina**, their version of So-and-so
or Whatsisname, or the American John and Jane Doe. Despite
appearances it has nothing to do with the **deinos** (strange, terri-
ble) that gives us 'dinosaur', which in turn has nothing to do with
the **dunamis** that gives us 'dynamite', which in turn has nothing
to do with the **odunē** that gives us 'anodyne'.

'His bodyweight' expands on the Greek original in an attempt at clarification. A big dictionary tells me an Attic talent was just over 26 kg, and an online source gives the average bodyweight of a European male as 70.8 kg: by that reckoning 'Mr A' pays out his own weight and then some. I am only moderately confident in my sums. Many classicists are bad at them, and ancient systems of reckoning do not help (**5.126**). What is more, the weight of a talent varied over time and in different places. In any case Philodemus is at least exaggerating for effect and may well have made up the whole scenario.

The Arabic number system we use today is great. Europeans started using it in the tenth century. It can support kinds of mathematics that would have daunted the Greeks, who were great ones for calculation but had no concept of zero. The names of Greek numbers live on in our geometric figures (geometry means earth-measurement)—pentagons, hexagons, and so on— and in monopods, bipods, tripods, and tesseracts. Unlikely as it sounds, the **-pod** in tripod is also the **-pous** in octopus (eight-foot) and Oedipus (Swell-foot, **9.166**)—but that story involves the third declension of Greek nouns (**6.254**), so let us leave it well alone for now. It's also why pedants such as myself insist that the plural of octopus ought to be *octopodes* or at least octopods, never *octopi*. Feel free to mock—we are ridiculous—but if they're going to be octopi, then we should be saying Antipi rather than *Antipodes* (Australians and New Zealanders are on the far side of the planet so their **podes** are opposite (**anti**) ours).

Romans represented figures through cumbersome combinations of a limited set of letters (I, V, X, L, D, C, M . . .), a system you could reverse-engineer if you were so inclined from the closing credits of BBC TV programmes. The Greeks had a different

solution: they got double value out of their whole alphabet by hav-
ing alpha equal 1, beta, 2, and so on, with a step up to increments
of ten at iota and of a hundred at rho, wrapping up at 800 with
omega before starting again at alpha with some extra squiggles.

This system can lead to confusion: is an odd-looking string
of letters a badly miscopied text, a magical formula, or some
arithmetic? But it also let people find hidden meanings in each
other's names by adding up the numerical values of their constit-
uent letters. MARKOS for instance is 40 + 1 + 100 + 20 + 70 + 200, a
total of 431, which might in turn be the sum total of the letters of
a word that meant 'lazy' or 'slow' or whatever. When the author
of the Book of Revelation declares that the Number of the Beast
is 666 (or in the earliest known papyrus copy, 616), he invites
readers to try to identify the Beast by doing just this kind of sum.
The practice is called *isopsephy* (**7.35**).

In case you were wondering, literal talent (a measure of mate-
rial resource) becomes figurative talent (an innate capacity) by
way of a New Testament parable, Matthew 25:14–30.

5.136 Meleager

Fill up my cup and say again, again,
'For Heliodora'. Say it one more time,
And mix that honeyed name into the brew,
The strong stuff, undiluted. Crown me too
With last night's garland, damp with scented oils
That still recall her presence. See, the rose,
The lover's friend, is weeping, for it sees
That she has gone away from my embrace,
Lies with another in another place.

5.137 The Same

Fill up my cup in Heliodora's name,
The Goddess of Persuasion; and one more
For Heliodora as the Cyprian,
And one last cup for the sweet-talking Grace
Who is that self-same girl: for she alone
Is reckoned as divinity by me,
Whose love-inducing name I swallow down
In place of water mixed with strongest wine.

Meleager gets drunk on love. An anonymous epigram recycles the second poem's basic idea of identifying the beloved as a Grace (of which there were three in myth), Muse (nine), and the one and only Aphrodite (5.95):

The Graces number four, the Paphians two;
There are ten Muses now, for Dercylis
Is Muse, and Grace, and also Paphian.

Persuasion was personified as Peitho, a close associate of Aphrodite. She was a long-established goddess whose genealogy is in Hesiod's *Theogony*, composed around the tail end of the eighth century BC. Other such personifications included Hypnos (Sleep)—the origin of our 'hypnosis', Thanatos (Death), Nemesis (Retribution) (**6.285**), Peitho's opposite number Bia (Force), and of course Aphrodite's naughty son, Erōs (Desire). The Greeks were fond of personifications and the roll-call grew over time. How they are represented depends on the grammatical gender of the abstract nouns that lie behind them. Many are feminine—Dikē (Justice), Alētheia (Truth), Tukhe (Fate, Latinized as *Tyche*), Eirēne (Peace), Nike (Victory and expensive running shoes), and so on.

The three Graces were women too, as were the Fates (the Parcae) and the Muses, whom Hesiod makes the daughters of Zeus and Memory.

Most people agreed there were nine Muses, but an alternative tradition that there were only three survived into the Roman Empire. Mostly they had to do with poetry, but not exclusively. The association of individual Muses with different forms of cultural display—Calliope for epic, Clio for history, Terpsichore for dance, and so on—seems to have developed in the Hellenistic age and was certainly unknown to the early audiences of Homer and Hesiod.

The imagined scene of these poems is a symposium, one that seems likely to go off the rails. Greeks were careful about how much they drank, or tried to be. They recognized the liberating power of Dionysus, god of the grape, and appreciated the power of wine to lower inhibitions and create a safe space for friends to speak plainly: the Latin saying *In vino veritas*, 'Truth in wine', has a Greek original behind it. But just as in matters of sex (**5.65**) they were also wary of taking it too far, losing control, and making a scene.

This was why symposiasts appointed one of their number as the evening's *symposiarch*. The -**arch** has to do with government: compare oligarchy, rule by a minority, and hierarchy, literally sacred rule; an architect is literally a boss builder. So the symposiarch was the literal master of ceremonies. He regulated the number of rounds of drink, and ruled on how much water should be added. Greeks always drank their wine mixed with water, in a broad vessel called a **kratēr**, for the shape of which are named volcanic craters and craters on the moon and other celestial bodies. Only barbarians or madmen took it neat. Greeks enjoyed their wine chilled, with snow or ice from the mountains when they could get it.

Astronomers often name craters after figures from myth. They are big fans of classical mythology, of science fiction (which raids classical mythology constantly), and often of both.

5.138 Dioscorides

Athēniōn sang *The Horse*, and brought me woe:
All Troy was burning; I too was aflame.
She scorched me, who had never learned to fear
The Grecians' ten-year siege. In that one blaze
Of the heroic past, Trojans and I
Were sunk together in calamity.

5.140 Meleager

The sweetly singing Muses with the harp;
Persuasion's sharp intelligence of mind;
Desire, that is your beauty's charioteer—
Zēnophila, they vested in your care
The sceptre of Desires, since Graces three
Endowed three graces as your property.

Dioscorides was a poet of the third century BC, two centuries before Meleager wove into his *Garland* those three-dozen poems of his that thereby survive so that we may read them. His name makes him a descendant of the *Dioscuri*, in Greek **Dioskouroi**, literally the sons of Zeus: Castor and Polydeuces (whom the

Romans called *Pollux*). This duo's conventional title papers over some inconsistency in the ancient accounts, which is par for the course: if there was one canonical version, it wouldn't be myth. Allegedly in one and the same night their mother Leda was impregnated both by her husband, Tyndareus, king of Sparta, and by Zeus in the guise of a swan. From this eventful coupling or throupling came also Helen—of Sparta, and then famously of Troy—and also Clytemnestra, whose revenge upon her unfaithful husband Agamemnon is the subject of Aeschylus' eponymous and very bloody tragedy.

Like Meleager, Dioscorides wrote epigrams expressing desire for young men and women alike. In this poem about a lovely boy (**12.37**) he again resorts to myth to get his point across:

> Sōsarchus of Amphipolis—that bum:
> Murderous Erōs played a nasty trick
> By moulding it as soft as marrowfat.
> He aimed to bother Zeus, because those thighs
> Are far more sweet than those of Ganymede.

Both the women in these poems from Book 5 are professional performers. We know that from the Hellenistic age onwards epigram found a home in the symposium, so readers of Meleager and Dioscorides are likely to have taken Athenion and Zenophila for **hetairai**. These socially and artistically skilled women made their way in the world as free agents by working as escorts. They were the exception to the symposium's men-only rule, because they were there in a professional capacity to perform music and be fascinating company.

On the three Graces see the immediately preceding poem, **5.137**, and also **5.146**, immediately following.

5.146 Callimachus

Four are the Graces: to the former three
A fourth has come, fresh from the sculptor's mould:
Berenice the blessed, beyond compare.
If she is lacking, Graces have not grace.

5.147 Meleager

White violet shall I weave, and weave as well
Gentle narcissus, myrtle running through,
And laughing lilies weave, and crocus sweet,
And plait the purple hyacinth, and weave
Roses, the lover's friends; that on the brows
Of Heliodora of the scented locks
My wreath may settle, scattering its blooms
Among the lovely tresses of her hair.

Two love poems that are more or less about something else. When Meleager sets out to plait a garland of flowers his readers cannot forget that he wove the *Garland* that was the Anthology's first great prototype, braiding his own poems (this one included) into it, and that to anthologize is to pick flowers for garlands (**5.81**). Ancient readers who met this poem as part of the *Garland* will have been primed by the collection's elaborate verse preface in which individual poets are assimilated to types of plant. Narcissus stood for Melanippides, a poet now entirely lost to us; myrtle, for Callimachus; lilies, Anyte (**6.312**), and crocus, Erinna (**7.13**); hyacinth, Alcaeus (**5.10**), roses, Sappho (**7.17**), and so on. At the start of the preface Meleager declares that he has woven this 'garland of poets' in honour of Diocles, a young man whom he desires. So we are in a world of poetry *about* poetry here, and the epigram to Heliodora invites a *metapoetic* reading.

Meleager wrote many epigrams to Heliodora: here is another, **5.143**:

> A garland rests on Heliodora's brow.
> It droops and fades, and yet the girl herself
> Blazes in brilliance, crowning her own crown.

Critics of the nineteenth and early twentieth centuries enjoyed spinning complex biographical stories that made her the love of Meleager's life, but he writes dozens of poems to other women as well (Zenophila of **5.177** is a particular favourite), and dozens more to cute young men. As noted, he dedicates his whole *Garland* to a special boyfriend. We come back to that poem at the end of this book.

Callimachus is working with similar material to Meleager **5.137**, but he has no romantic intentions towards Berenice. It would be a bad idea: she is his queen. The Ptolemaic dynasty that ruled Hellenistic Egypt (**7.39**) is a prosopographical mare's-nest of Ptolemies and Berenices; this one is Berenice II 'Euergetis' (Benefactress), wife of her half-cousin Ptolemy III in the mid-third century BC and a major political operator in her own right.

Callimachus wrote about her in two poetic fragments that survive on papyrus. Both are recognizably part of a programme of court propaganda in which Posidippus (**9.750**) was also heavily involved. One is a late example of *epinician* (**7.34–5**), poetry written to celebrate a sporting victory, in this case the first place won by her four-horse chariot team in the Nemean Games. The 'Milan Posidippus' papyrus published in 2001 includes a whole series

65

of epigrams about Berenice's racing victories. She was not the first royal woman to sponsor a race team—Cynisca of Sparta (her name means Puppy) famously won twice at the Olympics in the fifth century BC. The epigram from her victory monument survives, both in the Anthology (13.16) and on site:

> My fathers and my brothers: Spartan kings.
> My team of fleet-foot horses won their race,
> And I, Cynisca, set this statue here.
> I say I am the only champion
> Of all the women in the whole of Greece.

The other Callimachean fragment about Berenice is an account of *catasterism*, the elevation of a person to the stars above—or in this case, just a person's hair. The story went that Berenice vowed to cut off her hair as a votive offering to the gods if her husband should return safely from war. He returned and she fulfilled her vow, but the hair mysteriously vanished overnight from the temple in which it had been dedicated. Where could it have gone? The mystery was solved when the court astronomer Conon pointed out a new constellation in the night sky. To this day it is called the Lock of Berenice.

You are learning lots of words here that nobody will let you have in Scrabble, but you will never have the tiles for them anyway.

5.153 Asclepiades

> Nicarete had such a countenance,
> Complexioned by Desires, and only glimpsed
> Through upstairs windows; but the honeyed gaze

Of Cleophon who met her at the door
Has left it ashes. From his flashing eyes,
Dear Cyprian, the deadly lightning flies.

5.158 Asclepiades

Hermione is a persuasive girl.
I joined her in her game once, and she wore
A slender belt of delicate design—
Flowers, and golden writing that declared:
'Just love me anyway, and do not grieve
If he who keeps me is another man.'

Two poems about women as active players in the game of love,
by one of Book 5's best-represented poets. The speaker of the
first poem acknowledges Nicarete's own erotic capital, and notes
that her seclusion in the women's quarters of her father's tradi-
tional **oikos** (house and home) creates a mystique that makes
her beauty all the more enticing—but still he finds her charms
outdone by the sheer sexiness of young Cleophon. Nicarete has
fallen for him hopelessly and Asclepiades seems to feel the same
way, making this poem another uneasy fit in a book supposedly
devoted to heterosexual amours.

The Hermione of the second poem shares her name with the
mythical daughter of Helen and Menelaus of Sparta, and now
of course also with a character in *Harry Potter*. The Hermione of
myth was a niece of the Dioscuri (**5.140**) and married Orestes,
the son of Agamemnon; the Hermione of this epigram is having
a more interesting time. Like Athenion (**5.138**) and Xenophila
(**5.140**) she is by implication an escort. She is contracted to a

regular customer but is seeing Asclepiades behind that man's back.

When I write 'Asclepiades' I do not mean to say that I think the historically real poet Asclepiades necessarily lived these moments or knew these women, whose individual personalities probably never extended beyond these few elegiac couplets. Ancient poetry is not a sex diary or an album of emotions, and no one alive today has any pressing reason to care about whether Asclepiades was sad or horny on any particular day. Instead these little poems help us map out the contours of everyday experience within the culture he inhabited—or at least, they help tell us how everyday experience was mediated. In Hellenistic Egypt (his likely locale) as in every human time and place, people came to terms with their experiences and shared them around in ways that combine the seemingly timeless with the obviously local.

Hermione's belt is an intricate puzzle, by design. Within the scenario conjured up by the poem she must have had it made to order, an expensive treat to herself that exploits the wealth of her regular client while also declaring him an oblivious fool. Presumably he is not meant ever to find out what its motto says. Asclepiades' description of this unlikely belt is an example of *ekphrasis*, literally a 'talking-out', the description in literature (typically verse) of a real or imagined work of art. These ekphrases are characteristic of Alexandrian poetry of the early Hellenistic era. They draw on an already ancient Homeric template (for instance, the extended description of the shield of Achilles in Book 18 of the *Iliad*) but apply the technique to artworks that are as small and intricate as the poems that describe them, a *metapoetic* turn (compare **9.611**). Often the descriptions seem to mirror back onto the poems and to be saying something about their larger themes, but the question of *what* they might be saying is left for the individual reader to decipher as best they can.

The Greek **oikos** was a productive unit as much as a family one: produce was stored there, and crafts plied, notably weaving. The Greek word **oikonomia**, meaning the running of such a household with a view to keeping it in the black, is still with us as 'economy'.

5.164 Asclepiades

I call you as my witness, lady Night,
You and no other, how she brings me shame—
Nico's girl, Pythias. It is her way
To tease and trick: she called me and I came;
I was not uninvited. So may she
Endure the same and loiter at my door,
And curse at you for what she did before.

5.167 Asclepiades

Rainy it was, and night, and for the third
Of lovers' pains, I had been taking wine;
Chilly north wind as well. and I alone,
And lovely Moschus had the upper hand:
'The state of you! Please be upon your way,
And do not dally before just one door.'
Drenched as I was, I bellowed: 'Zeus, how long?!—
But Zeus, my friend, you need not answer, sure;
You too have known what lovers must endure.'

If you want to impress your friends, but will be every bit as happy to confuse and alienate them, then I have the perfect word for you: **paraklausithuron**. You pronounce it just like it's written. Try it now: **para–klausi** (rhymes with lousy)–**thuron**. Six syllables of joy. It may be inspired by a pretty young man or woman—Asclepiades has weaknesses for both—and you might meet it Latinized as *paraclausithyron*, with *c* and *y* for **k** and **u** (**5.34**). However you encounter it, those six syllables translate as 'beside—a closed—door'. The song of the shut-out lover is a favourite trope of erotic epigram because moping is its stock in trade. Very often rain is falling to match the mood. The motif is there right from the start of literary epigram, and Asclepiades is there when it happens. Later, Propertius and Ovid bring it over into their Latin love elegies as the *exclusus amator*.

The Anthology's **paraklausithura** are the all-too-frequent conclusion of a drunken **kōmos** (**5.64**) through the night-time streets. The disappointed lover has come garlanded from a symposium and often leaves his wilting wreath hanging at the gate-post of that stubbornly barred and guarded door, in the hope that the object of his ~~nuisance~~ affections may see it in the morning and soften a little towards him. Here is one such by Meleager, three hundred years later (**5.190**):

> I ask you, stars, and you, the Moon that shines
> So brightly for us lovers, and the lyre
> That wanders with us in our revelling:
> That wicked girl now lying in her bed—
> Will I arrive to find her chasing sleep,
> Sobbing her woes, the lamp alone to hear,
> Or is she with another man again?
> Then I shall hang my garlands soaked with tears

As prayer-offerings upon her door,
With only this small caption to explain:
'Cyprian, in whose secret revelries
I am conscripted, Meleager here
Hangs up these trophies, stripped from love new-slain.'

Asclepiades' Pythias and Meleager's unnamed 'girl' are by clear implication **hetairai**, escorts; the poem doesn't dwell on it, but Nico must be Pythias' pimp. Moschus is not an escort, but he is no better than he ought to be, as our grandmothers might have said. He will doubtless do well in politics one day.

5.169 Nossis

'Nothing's more sweet than Love; all precious things
Come second to it; honey from my mouth
I spat out, even.' So does Nossis say:
But if a woman has not known the kiss
Of Aphrodite, then I say that she
Is ignorant which flower is the rose.

Nossis was a third-century poet of Epizephyrean Locris in what is now Reggio Calabria, right down in the toe of Italy's boot, and called after the west wind (Zephyr, **6.53**) to distinguish it from a Locris back in the old country. The Greeks colonized the coast of southern Italy early on, with the consequence that the Romans first got to grips with Greek culture in encounters with their neighbours in what they (the Romans) called *Magna Graecia*, 'Great(er) Greece'. The Greeks were great coastal wanderers and their seaports have endured: Marseilles began as one of theirs, and so did Naples, founded as *Neapolis*, New City.

Antipater of Thessalonica (9.26) ranked Nossis as one of antiquity's nine great women poets:

> Helicon raised these women up with song,
> And made their tongues divine: Pieria too,
> The Muses' rocky crag in Macedon.
> PRAXILLA; MOERO; ANYTE, in voice
> A female Homer; SAPPHO too, the pride
> Of Lesbian women with their lovely hair;
> ERINNA; TELESILLA, of great fame;
> And you, CORINNA, who once danced and sang
> Athena's war-shield; NOSSIS, woman-tongued;
> Sweet-sounding MYRTO—all the workwomen
> Of ever-living pages. Muses nine
> Did great Olympus bear, and Earth nine too,
> Immortal merriment for all mankind.

There had to be nine, to match the nine Muses. Similarly there was a canon of nine great archaic lyric poets—Archilochus, Alcaeus, and so on. Nine was a favourite number for this kind of thing; seven was good, too (Seven Wonders, Seven Sages). Sappho is the only poet to appear in both the lyric lists. Nossis came after her, and her poetry announces her intention to rival Sappho's genius.

Fragments of Telesilla's lyric songs survive: her home city, Argos, revered her as a poet and patriot. According to local lore, when Sparta laid siege to Argos after slaughtering its menfolk at the Battle of Sepeia (494 BC) she led the city's women to the walls and beat the invaders back. Erinna is known for her *Distaff*, a poem of women's craft and girls' friendship of which a large fragment has been discovered on papyrus (**7.13**); Anyte is represented in this collection (**6.132**). The poems of Corinna, a choral poet of the cattle-country of Boeotia, survive in fragments but her name is now more familiar as that of the probably fictional girlfriend in Ovid's Latin love elegies. the *Amores*.

5.177 Meleager

Public announcement of a runaway:
The boy called Love, a savage little thing,
Who just this very minute took to wing
At daybreak from our bed. Appearance thus:
Sweet in his tears, forever tattling,
Quick-moving, fearless, with a knowing smile.
As to his father's name, I cannot say:
No one can tell me, but it was not Sky,
Nor was the Earth his parent, nor the Sea,
To hear the story. What a wicked boy!
Everyone hates him, everywhere you go,
So check with care he is not setting lines
To trap the hearts of others even now.
But wait—look! There he is, beside his lair.
Boy with the bow, I caught you by surprise,
Who hid yourself in Zenophila's eyes.

Meleager addresses many epigrams to Zenophila, rather spoiling the game of gentlemanly nineteenth-century critics who wanted to declare Heliodora the poet's one true love (the Myiscus poems they tended to pass over in silence, **12.65**). This poem and its sequel in the Anthology develop the trope of Erōs as a slave. Picturing Aphrodite's divine brat as unfree is an unexpected twist on the motif of love as a form of enslavement—normally Erōs is the one dishing that stuff out. The reader is meant to be amused.

73

Slavery in real life was no joke, though regarded universally as a fact of life. Stoics (**5.93**) warned against becoming a slave to one's passions, which you'd think ought to mean slavery was a Bad Thing, but no philosopher ever proposed its abolition: that some people owned others was basic to how the world worked. In times of conquest enslavement could be a consequence of defeat (**6.171**) but most slaves were bred, just like domesticated animals were bred; citizens could be fond of them and rely on them, just as they were fond of animals that did their jobs right (**6.176**), recognizing their humanity in the abstract while relying on their compelled labour every day of their lives (**5.183–5**). Cherished slave children could be fussed over as pets, or be used in ways you don't want to think about.

True, even the great Heracles had spent time as a slave (**6.138**), and it did not have to be a life sentence (**7.17, 12.93**); some (skilled staff) had it better than others (labourers); many worked alongside free citizens; some former slaves prospered in commerce and their children had the same rights as anyone else's, but none of that makes it alright. No wonder slaves often ran away, despite the high likelihood of recapture and harsh punishment. Often a recaptured runaway would be branded on the forehead, announcing their wickedness to the world and making it all but impossible to build a new life if they ran again.

Meleager's 'public announcement of a runaway' follows a template familiar from mundane examples found on papyrus. He tells us the slave's name (he would say who the father was as well if he could) and also, crucially, what the boy looks like. The fugitives of real-life public notices are always identified by a detailed physical description that specifies any marks and scars—and there usually were marks and scars, because the ancient world

74

had rough edges and a slave could not effectively protect a body they did not own.

One source of young slaves was unwanted infants. Not every parent could afford to feed another mouth, or a new baby might have an evident disability. Such babies were discarded or sold. In the sequel epigram (5.178) Meleager comes into Zenophila's room to find her asleep, and the infant Erōs with her. Though he calms down after, his immediate reaction is to get what he can for the ugly little blighter:

> Let it be sold! Though yet it is asleep
> On mother's breast. What use is it to me
> To raise up such a brat? Look at its nose! ...

5.183 Posidippus

> We will be four at the symposium,
> And each comes with a girlfriend, making eight;
> One Chian will not do. So, little boy,
> Go over to Aristion's, and say
> The one he sent the first time was half-full;
> Twelve pints are missing, for a certainty,
> And I'd say more. Go quickly as you can:
> By five our party will be under way.

5.185 Asclepiades

> Go to the marketplace, Demetrius,
> And ask Amyntas for some bluefish, three,
> Ten little wrasse that live among the weed,

And get two dozen hunchback shrimp as well—
He'll count them out for you. As you come home
Pick up six rose-wreaths from Thauborias . . .
And pop in too, since it's along your way,
To see if Tryphera can come and play.

Two slaves are sent out shopping, one for an amphora of the wine-merchant's finest, the other for fish and woven garlands, both of which had to be fresh on the day. Between them they will have the makings of dinner (**deipnon**) and the separate drinking-party that follows (**sumposion**). Romans at dinner (*cena*) drank while they ate, but Romans were peculiar. Posidippus plans on starting the evening early: the fifth hour was the tail end of the working day, typically with a nap to follow. Remember that day and night were each divided into twelve hours, the lengths of which varied with the seasons (**5.7**).

The wine of Chios was one of the acknowledged greats and known to be good for you. Greeks planted vines wherever they settled, including the south of France and southern Italy, called by them **Oinotria**, the Land of Wine. Even before Rome the international wine trade was vast, shipping wine long distances in big clay amphorae that were broken down at destination into smaller jars for the retail trade. There's a very good 'Ancient Greece and wine' Wikipedia page about it all. As for fish, it was the gourmet's choice at table, with game in second place. Both took skill and patience to acquire; game had some prestige because hunting was part of the young aristocrat's skillset for Greeks and Romans alike (**6.114**), but in an era before rail and refrigeration it was hard for an urban chef to source really fresh fish, lending it scarcity value. Other meats were eaten, to be sure, but nobody put a premium on steak: cows were for milk, and bulls for pulling ploughs (**6.55**) and carts. Where was the glamour in eating tractor?

If you want to put yourself in the party-shoes of an ancient gourmet I can recommend Andrew Dalby's *Empire of Pleasures* (the man knows his food and drink) and for classical Athens James Davidson's *Courtesans and Fishcakes*, which I always think would be a terrific title for a tabletop roleplaying game, like *Dungeons and Dragons* but more delicious in every way. The courtesan Tryphera, whose working name sells her talents as a good-time girl (**truphē** is luxury, refinement, sensuality), would make an excellent NPC.

I won't drag you far into ancient weights, measures, and prices. Ancient Greek wallets held silver drachmas and bronze obols. In classical Athens a skilled worker or a hoplite on active service earned a drachma a day; Athenian drachmas were popular far and wide, their silver mined by state-owned slaves (**5.177**), but every city-state minted its own coinage. There were four-drachma coins as well ('tetradrachms'—**tetra** means four, as in tetrahedron) and Hellenistic rulers came up with bigger multi-drachma coins to show off how fancy they were. Romans had silver *denarii* and bronze *sestertii*, on similar lines to drachmas and obols. There was inflation, but nobody understood it, or they kept quiet if they did: rising prices just went to show that merchants were a greedy lot. Greeks measured handily in finger-joints (dactyls), feet, and cubits; for longer distances, stades (as in stadium!) and some chain measures borrowed from Egypt and Persia. Romans of course had their mile, for *milia passum*, a thousand Roman feet. The standard Roman foot was just a fraction shorter than our own; if it was a real foot it would take a UK size twelve.

5.186 Posidippus

Do not imagine you can pull the wool
Across my eyes with simulated tears,
However lifelike: for I know your game.
I know you love nobody more than me,
Not in the world, Philaenis, for as long
As we are bedmates; if another man
Were paying for you, you would up and swear
You loved him more than ever you did me.

5.187 Meleager

Say to Philaenis, Dorcas: 'You should know
Your crime has been found out. Each golden kiss
Was counterfeit; base alloy lay within.
Time has revealed your love as forgery.'

Two lovers affronted that a working girl is what she is. At **6.206** an identically named hetaira gives thanks to Aphrodite, the patron goddess of her calling, for a lucrative career. That poem is by Antipater of Sidon, a much later poet than Posidippus and Meleager. Is it the same Philaenis? Maybe yes and no. Philaenis is a stock name for a hetaira in epigram and was doubtless also a frequent working name taken by sex workers in the real world of the Hellenistic Mediterranean. Philaenis was also named as the author of an ancient sex manual—with pictures!—of which, alas, only an introductory fragment survives, so hers was a name to conjure with, like Mrs Beeton's for cookbooks back in the day. Though more than a century separates Posidippus and Meleager from Antipater, the imaginative world of erotic epigram has not changed a bit: always there is a Philaenis.

Dorcas in Meleager's poem is Philaenis' maid. She might be an employee, or a slave (**5.177**). In erotic epigram these maids are confidants and go-betweens, and the wise lover will take care to stay in their good books. Dorcas means 'She who sees' everything that goes on, from the same irregular Greek verb that gives us the treasure-guarding **drakōn** (dragon). A few poems previously in the book Meleager had addressed another such epigram to the same Dorcas, betraying his eagerness to arrange an assignation (**5.182**):

> Take her this message, Dorcas, and be sure
> You tell the whole thing over and again.
> Run now, and stay no longer. Fly away!—
> But wait a moment, Dorcas, if you will;
> Where are you rushing too, before you hear
> All of my message? Tell her what I said
> The other time, and say as well—but why
> Am I so silly? Really you need say
> Nothing at all, except that—tell her all;
> No holding back, tell her the whole damn thing.
> Come to that, Dorcas, why should I send you,
> When I can come along and lead the way?

Since then the relationship has soured, and the closeness between the two poems invites readers to fill in the gap with their own imaginings, much as readers of modern comics and graphic novels mentally fill in what is happening in the gutters between the panels. The gold of Philaenis' kisses was a thin veneer over something much nastier; her love was **plastos**, malleable and artificial, from a Greek root that gives us plastic and plasma. Or so says the Meleagrian lover, a sore loser who wants something other than what she was selling; the followers of Epicurus (**5.93**) would have told him to pay, enjoy, and move on.

5.228 Paul the Silentiary

For whom now will you curl and cut your hair,
Or manicure your hands and trim your nails?
Towards what end will you adorn your gowns
With ocean-bloom of murex, since no more
Can you attend on lovely Rhodope?
I cannot look on Rhodope, and so
I do not care that these my eyes should see
Even the golden light of shining morn.

5.247 Macedonius the Consul

Your name is Parmenis, for Constancy;
A fitting name, I thought when first I heard,
But you have made a lie of it, and now
I hate you more than death. You shun the man
Who cares for you, and set your sights instead
Upon the man who does not—just until
He takes his turn at falling, so that you
Can shun *him*, too. Your kiss is like a hook,
Spurring to madness, and I took the bait;
And now from rosy lips I hang and wait.

Two girls with names that tell on them, like Tryphera's in **5.185**: Rhodope is rosy-faced, and Parmenis is Constance, except when she isn't.

The tail end of Book 5 is dominated by these two poets. Paul and Macedonius come to the Anthology by way of the Cycle of Agathias, an anthology of contemporary epigram compiled by a lawyer at Constantinople in the sixth century AD under the Emperor Justinian I. Macedonius was an honorary consul with the Greek title **Hupatos** or Highest, a bit less important than it sounds; Paul kept order and silence at court under the Latin title *Silentarius* or Usher ('hush!'), a lot more important than it sounds. So these poets were senior civil servants, not lovesick symposiasts about to venture out on a **kōmos** to the door of a cold-hearted boy or girl. They were also Christians, but like other men of their class they were classically educated. Their poems do a fine job of imaginatively reanimating a lost world of pagan pleasure that had faded away long before.

Two centuries before them, the bitter epigrammatist Palladas of Alexandria had mourned the passing of the old order (10.82):

> Are we not dead and only seem to live,
> We pagan men, fallen disastrously
> Into a dream we only think is life?
> Or do we live, and life itself has died?

But there was still plenty of life in the fantasy, and perhaps it had always been more fantasy than anything else. We have the New Rome in the east to thank for curating and preserving practically all the ancient Greek literature that survived through multiple manuscript copies long enough to meet the age of print. The remains of the western Empire had forgotten their Greek long before, and knew authors such as Homer and Sappho only by reputation. From the twelfth century Western monks and scholars could again read Aristotle but only because his works had come to them in Latin translations—some of them straight out of the Greek and made in Byzantium, others based on Arabic intermediaries.

Agathias, the Cycle's compiler, had trained at the great Roman legal school of Berytus, our Beirut (see **13.7**); he was an expert public speaker who played some part in local politics but was best known as a poet and historian. We have a hundred or so of his own epigrams and they are very good indeed.

BOOK 6

THE DEDICATIONS

6.10 Antipater <of Thessalonica>

Trito-born Pallas, goddess who defends,
Daughter of Zeus who flees the marriage-bond,
Unwedded and unchildbirthed queen—to you
Seleucus raised this altar made of horns,
When the mouth issued a Phoebean cry.

There once was a very famous altar made of horn, one of the
Seven Wonders of the Ancient World in some lists; it was dedi-
cated to Artemis in her great sanctuary at Delos, so this is not it.
'Seleucus' could be the historically famous founder of the Seleucid
dynasty, or one-or-other of his numerous and eponymous descend-
ants, or any of various other well-known Seleucuses besides
(Wikipedia disambiguates them, https://en.wikipedia.org/wiki/
Seleucus); or some other, less attested person of that name.

Pallas is Athena, whose frequent epithet **Tritogeneia**, 'Triton-
born', is variously explained. It is given here in a rarer form,
Tritogenēs. Indeed the whole poem is a treasury of weird words:
Denys Page in *Further Greek Epigram* (1982) points out the epithets

A Book of Greek Life: The Ancient World Through Epigram. Gideon Nisbet, Oxford University Press.
© Gideon Nisbet 2026. DOI: 10.1093/oso/9780198994756.003.0003

phugiodemnios ('who flees the marriage-bond') and **apeiro-tokos**, the rare-bird qualities of which I try to echo with 'unchild-birthed'.

Greek is a concise language, and epigrams were written by masters of concision. My version runs to five lines; the original has four, that is to say, two elegiac couplets. One of the things I like about this poem is that nobody knows what to do with its closing line. Why would an altar to Athena be built at the urging of Phoebus Apollo, and whose mouth is it? The German school-teacher Hugo Stadtmüller, who edited the Anthology for the Teubner press in the 1890s, sidestepped the problem by suggest-ing that two lines had dropped out of the text just before the end; the original would have run to three elegiac couplets, not two, and the missing pentameter and hexameter would have made everything run smoothly. Subsequent scholarship ran variations on the theme. Paton's Loeb posited the loss from the end of the poem of a third couplet that would have filled in the rest of the mouth's story; Page hypothesized as an alternative that the origi-nal last line of the poem had been lost, and that the line trans-mitted in the manuscript had wandered in from another poem entirely.

I wonder if the 'mouth' (**stoma**) might not be the mouth of a cave or chasm; we do find the Greek word used for those. I ten-tatively suggest that, whoever the Seleucus was who built this horned altar, he did so in response to an oracle issued at Delphi. Vapours from a chasm there inspired the utterances of Apollo's priestess, the Pythia. If so, the poem is alluding with typical epi-grammatic concision to a fuller story that is otherwise lost to us—lost, that is, as far as I know.

6.24 <Anonymous>

This woven net worn out, but worn in vain,
Does Heliodorus hang as offering
Here in the temple porch for Syria's Queen.
Guiltless of blood it was in fishery;
Instead it gathered countless strands of wrack,
Piling it high upon the friendly shore.

Plenty of dedicatory epigrams concern fishermen and their gear. In addition to the many variants on the theme of 'three brothers' who hunt with nets by land, sea, and air (6.11–16 and 179–87), there is a substantial run of fishing poems at 6.23–30. In epigrams on trades and crafts generally, the typical occasion for dedicating tools is retirement after a successful career, but that expectation can also be subverted.

Astarte or Ishtar was an ancient goddess whose worship was widespread across the Near East from prehistoric times. The Egyptians knew her, and the Phoenicians spread her worship as far as Spain by the eighth century BC. Our fullest literary source for her cult is an essay titled *On the Syrian Goddess* by the second-century sophist ('wise guy', pundit), Lucian of Samosata. His reasons for writing it are unclear; he is a tricky author who often debunks religious silliness, but he also frequently expresses pride in his native identity as Syrian or Assyrian. Here is part of his account of Astarte's cult at Hierapolis. Lions were sacred to her:

> In the great court oxen of great size browsed; horses, too, are there, and eagles and bears and lions, who never hurt mankind but are all sacred and all tame. (41)

Under her miraculous protection at Hierapolis, at least according to Lucian, humans and animals lived alongside one another, doing and suffering no harm. I suppose this makes her a fit dedicatee for a fishing-net that was never any good for catching fish.

For all his failure as a fisherman, Heliodorus may still have scraped a living by his net. Seaweed was gathered and fermented to produce the purplish-red dye orchil, used for rouge, and called **phukos** just like the wrack from which it was made. When the misogynistic satirist Lucillius at 11.310 critiques a woman's purchase of expensive cosmetics—'For that amount you might have bought a face'—orchil is on his list.

You can read Lucian's essay on Astarte in an old translation by Herbert Strong and John Garstang, available online (https://www.sacred-texts.com/cla/luc/tsg/tsg07.htm).

The poem's authorship and date are unknown. I do not imagine a connection with the Syrian Heliodorus who wrote the *Aethiopica* in the third or fourth century AD, though I highly recommend that tricky and engrossing novel.

6.37 Anonymous

It too is stooped with age: this beechwood bough
The herders of the mountain pasture cut,
Shaved off its bark, and set it up for Pan
Upon the road, a handsome ornament
For the protector of the yearling droves.

6.55 John Barbocallus

This cottage cheese and beehive honeycomb
Eurynomus the oxherd, freshly wed,
Offers to Peitho and the Paphian;
But count the cheese as offered for her sake,
And know the gift of honey is from me.

Two pastoral offerings. The obvious real or imagined context for an epigram marking a dedication is a god's temple or sacred precinct, but Pan is not one to be penned in. The droves are an instance of translator's liberty: the Greek just says herds (**boukolia**), but these are herdsmen who pasture their cattle in the high places, practising transhumance. They drive their herds and flocks up in the spring and down again in autumn. Go up to those same Mediterranean mountain pastures at the right time of year and you will see their descendants doing the same today. And wolves are a threat to livestock in those pastures still.

Then as now, subsistence farming was hard work. The *pastoral* dream of carefree herdsmen piping tunes in the shade took form in Alexandria in Egypt, a Hellenistic megacity that made the Rome of its day look small and backward; actual herdsmen have no such illusions. Pastoral is the genre's Latin name, from *pastor*, a shepherd (hence pastors in churches); you may also see it called *bucolic*, from **boukolos**, an oxherd. **Bous** is ox; the Latin is *bos*, from which we get bovine and Bovril (the -vril bit is from a Victorian science-fiction novel by the author of *The Last Days of Pompeii*). A document in which the lines are written alternately from left to right and right to left is said to be written **boustrophedon**, the writer switching direction at each line-end like a plough-ox at the end of each furrow. Again, unfeasible in Scrabble.

John Barbocallus was a Christian poet of the Byzantine Empire, and the pagan idyll of his epigram is a nostalgic literary fiction reminiscent of Theocritus' *Idylls*. 'The Paphian' is a common enough cult epithet of Aphrodite, and Peitho, Persuasion personified (**5.137**), is often invoked with her as a lover's helper. Eurynomus has cause to thank them both, and by keeping them sweet (honey is by far the better gift, **5.32**) he keeps his future options open. I note that his bride does not get a name.

The few surviving epigrams of Barbocallus show considerable range. He wrote two poems on the city of Berytus in Libya, which I think must have been his home. One (16.38) celebrates its deliverance in battle from Byzantium's great enemy, the Sassanid Persians, in an unlikely victory led by a local scholar; the other (9.427) laments its total destruction by earthquake and fire not long afterwards: see note on **13.7**.

6.53 Bacchylides

Eudemus raised this temple on his farm
To the most fattening of all the winds,
The Zephyr, that came rushing to his prayer,
That he might quickly winnow his return
Out of the corn-sheaves ripened by the sun.

6.114 Philip of Thessalonica

Hide of an ox, and horns a fathom wide:
A royal gift, high in the porch we hang
Of Heracles, son of Amphitryo.

We are a present fourteen handspans long.
The braggart beast met Philip in the fight;
His dreadful spear-throw cast it to the ground,
Hard below Orbelus where cattle roam.
Emathia is richly blessed indeed,
Ruled as it is by such a general.

Two votive dedications from the Greek countryside.

In the forum that the Romans added to post-conquest Athens there is a famous octagonal tower, the Tower of the Winds. It is much imitated: the Radcliffe Observatory in Oxford and St Pancras' Church in London are two examples among many. The tower had eight sides because there were eight winds, one for each compass-point. The most celebrated are Boreas (the north wind), Eurus (the south-east or east), Notus (the south), and Zephyrus (the west). Each had its characteristic weather and season: Boreas was the god of foul winter weather and was depicted accordingly as a sturdy fellow in a cloak; Zephyr inaugurated spring, nurtured young plants, and aided lovers; Notus was the dry sirocco out of Africa who brought withering heat and destructive storms in late summer and early autumn, the time of year called 'dog-days' for the heliacal rising of the dog-star, Sirius; and so on.

Thessalonica is in Macedonia or Macedon (the ancient kingdom is called either interchangeably), and Orbelus was a mighty mountain on the border between Macedon and Thrace. The wooded glens beneath such a range are great country for hunters. Emathia was one of Macedon's provinces, and Greek and Roman poets used its name as a synonym for the kingdom as a whole because it was much easier to scan (the rhetorical term for this device is *synecdoche*). The Philip of the poem is not its scholarly author (first century AD), but a celebrated fellow-countryman who lived long before his time: Philip II (382–336), the king who bloodily unified first his own kingdom and then all of Greece, planning to lead it in an invasion of Persia to redress historic wrongs. He was assassinated before he could begin his campaign, but his son Alexander III carried it through—and then kept going, through the Stans and all the way to north-western India. This swathe of slaughter would eventually see him called 'the Great'.

The mighty wild ox that Philip slew was surely an aurochs; there were still plenty of them about, and a king would hardly have been chasing after some random bull. For Greeks and Romans alike, and indeed for Persians, hunting was an aristo-cratic pursuit and always had been, especially if the quarry was dangerous. The Emperor Hadrian and his beautiful younger lover Antinous hunted a rogue lion together in Egypt in AD 130 before their fateful voyage up the Nile; a fragment of a papyrus book-roll from Oxyrhynchus preserves part of an epic poem written by a Greek-Egyptian poet called Pancrates to celebrate Hadrian's prowess, very much as Philip's epigram declares the bravery and skill of his famous namesake.

Speaking of Pancrates, an excellent epigram under that name appears very shortly afterwards in the Anthology (6.117). Lame Hephaestus was the divine smith of Olympus:

> The hammer, crab-claw pincer, and the tong.
> Warm from the forge, they hang as offerings
> To lord Hephaestus from Polycrates,
> The tools with which he hammered constantly
> Upon his anvil, leaving for his sons
> A rich inheritance, and beating back
> With constant force the pain of poverty.

6.124 Hegesippus

Timanōr's bloody shoulders bore me once,
And now, a shield, I hang beneath the eaves
Of Pallas' shrine, Defender in the Fight.
I often knew the dust of iron war,
And ever warded death from him who bore.

6.127 Nicias

Just like the others, I was always bound
To leave behind the hateful strife of War
And listen to the chorus of the girls
Beside the shrine of Artemis, the place
Where Epixenus dedicated me,
When pale old age began to sap his limbs.

Two dedications of shields, hung up by professional soldiers. Mercenaries were a staple of ancient Greek warfare, and never more so than in the early Hellenistic age. They left their mark on the up-and-coming genres of new comedy (Plautus' *Miles Gloriosus* is a mercenary recruiter) and epigram. Book 6 of the Anthology preserves many poems in which veterans hang up their well-used gear as they retire on the profit of a trade almost constantly in demand. Here is another such, by Mnasalcas (**6.264**):

The shield of Alexander, Phylleus' son,
I hang here as a holy offering
To lord Apollo of the golden hair.
Worn is my rim and tired by constant war,
Worn too my boss, but courage makes me shine,

Courage I earned in arming that brave man
Who set me here. From when I first was made,
I never have been worsted or outdone.

Doubtless plenty of real-life mercenaries did make offerings on retirement to whatever deity they credited for keeping them alive, and these will have been fit occasions for commissioning inscriptions, a minority of which were surely in verse. Many versions from the Anthology, though, are part of an extended conversation (which may nonetheless have intersected with and enriched actual inscriptional practice) between literary authors. Nicias' poem implicitly acknowledges that plenty of poets have tried their hand at the 'shield' trope already ('just like the others')—and Nicias comes very early in epigram's development as a literary genre. He was a doctor by profession but also a poet of note, and the first great pastoral poet (**6.55**), Theocritus, addresses a poem to him (*Idyll* 11, 'The Cyclops') as a friend and fellow talent whose medical training gives him special understanding of the pains of love. We might choose to see that echoed in the way the shield of his poem reflects on its retirement from a world of war to one of young women coming together to dance and sing songs of each other's beauty.

There was nothing unusual about men dedicating weapons and armour in temples to goddesses; Athena was a particular favourite. Artemis too was sometimes depicted with shield and spear, and Pausanias tells us that the Athenians and Spartans sacrificed to her as Agrotera (Huntress) for good fortune in war. But Artemis was also the virgin protector of young animals and was especially important in the lives of young girls. At Brauron in Attica, Athenian girls attended an annual camp at which they turned into bears, embracing their animal side in a ritual the details of which are not remotely known.

6.132 Nossis

Bruttian soldiers cast these arms away
From shoulders fated to a sorry end,
Falling beneath the blows of Locrians—
Keen fighters, of whose courage they now sing,
Hanging within the temples of the gods,
And do not miss the forearms of those men,
The cowards they forsook and left behind.

This epigram by a professional woman poet of Magna Graecia in the third century BC (**5.169**) is written to accompany a trophy of captured arms set up by her fellow-citizens after a decisive victory against a native Italian tribe. The Greek colonists who came to southern Italy in the archaic period staked a claim to prime coastal sites with fertile plains behind them, often at river mouths, and pushed the Italic locals inland. The Bruttii were one such people in what is now Calabria. Nossis supplies the inscriptional voice through which the captured shields can sing aloud in praise of the Greeks who took them as booty.

At around the same time Leonidas of Tarentum (AP 6.129) was celebrating a very similar victory just down the road, against another and closely neighbouring Oscan-speaking people of the Italian hinterland. This one was won with help from Tarentum's mother city, Sparta, and one of the victors hung up his loot in a sanctuary back in Spartan home territory:

Eight shields, eight helms, eight linen coats-of-mail,
As many blood-stained cleavers: all this gear
Hagnon, Euanthes' son, mighty in war,
Offers as spoil from the Lucanians,
Athena's now, at Coryphasium.

History did not treat the Lucanians well; their legacy today extends no further than the Greek word for sausages, **loukanika**.

Shields are cumbersome objects and very heavy. Anyone trying to run from a battlefield would need to throw theirs away; hence the famous injunction of Spartan women to their menfolk to come back either with their shields (victorious), or on them (dead). Our source for that saying is Plutarch, a Greek of the first century AD who hailed from Chaeronea in the Peloponnese and whose vast body of work includes the collected famous sayings of Spartan men and women alike. All such utterances were laconic by definition: Laconic means 'of Laconia', which in turn means Spartan. Losing a shield was doubly shameful because it lent protection not just to its bearer, but even more so to the men standing beside him in the *phalanx*. This close-packed block of *hoplites* (literally shieldmen) was a tough nut so long as everyone played their part, but if it broke, the slaughter could be terrible.

The ideology of the phalanx was centuries old, and was open to question since its beginning. It was hard to beat on the open plain but a liability on chancy ground, and the Greek heartland has a very high ratio of chancy ground to open plain. Here is Archilochus, in a surviving elegiac fragment from the seventh century BC, translated by Martin West for the World's Classics:

> Some Saian sports my splendid shield.
> I had to leave it in a wood,
> But saved my skin. Well, I don't care—
> I'll get another just as good.

Nossis seems every bit as keen on war as are her fellow poets of Greek Italy, at least when her side is winning. This is by no means her only epigram written to accompany a martial dedication. The adjective that I translate as 'keen fighters', **ōkumakhos**, is found only in this poem and may be her own coinage.

6.135 'Anacreon'

Phidolas' horse from Corinth's open plain
Stands here as offering to Kronos' son,
A lasting witness to the mighty pace
Of drumming feet with which he won the race.

6.136 The Same

This dress was fashioned by Frēxidice,
Designed by Dyseris: two of a kind
Who share a genius for industry.

6.138 'Anacreon'

Calliteles had me erected here,
In time gone by—but *this*, his progeny
Raised up, so grant them favour in return.

Three epigrams attributed to the archaic lyric poet Anacreon, with added scare-quotes. None of them can be by him, because epigram didn't exist outside inscriptions when he was around (**5.80**) and wouldn't for another couple of hundred years. These anonymous epigrams were a kind of literary game. Readers and listeners enjoyed them for what they were, and were not fooled.

A BOOK OF GREEK LIFE

We know ancient partygoers enjoyed songs of love and wine that were Anacreon-*ish* (**7.23**), and didn't worry overmuch about the boundaries of strictly historical authorship. What's a little odd about the Anthology's pseudo-Anacreontic epigrams is that they sit outside that tradition of drinking, wenching, and whatever the word is for wenching when it's boys. These are dedicatory poems of a chaste and sober kind. They caption a statue of a horse, offered to Zeus at the sacred site of the Olympic Games where it won its owner a crown of olive-boughs (**12.65**), with echoes of Homeric diction (*Iliad* 20.411); a lovely dress, dedicated by implication in a sanctuary of Athena who was patron of crafts and of weaving in particular; and . . . *something* offered to *some* god, *somewhere*. That last one is a puzzle and we've no idea what to do with it. Classics is like that sometimes.

Let me take your mind off it with another pretty frock. This epigram is by one Diotimus (meaning Honoured by Zeus), and like the 'Anacreon' poems it is written as though to accompany a temple offering. Diotimus calls the dress a **kupassis**, a mini-dress that reaches to mid-thigh, befitting an active young woman with a barbarian's sense of modesty (**6.358**):

> Hello, you dainty frock, that Omphale
> The Lydian girl once shed as she embarked
> Upon her love-affair with Heracles.
> You were a lucky little garment then,
> And your luck held a second time, that day
> You reached this golden hall of Artemis.

Did you know that the heroic career of Hercules (to give him his more familiar Roman name) included a sissy-maid episode? It's all true. Omphale was a legendary queen of Lydia, a kingdom encompassing modern Turkey and more (Herodotus tells how it was later ruled by Croesus of legendary wealth and fell to the Medes, becoming part of the Persian Empire that in the fifth century invaded Greece and was repulsed at Marathon, Salamis, and Plataea (**7.39**)). To atone for an accidental manslaughter, Heracles was ordered by the Delphic Oracle to spend a year as Omphale's slave. She dressed him in women's clothing and he spent the year doing women's work in her palace, helping with weaving and such; Omphale meanwhile appropriated his lion-skin, the original boyfriend jeans. Heracles doesn't seem to have minded one bit, and he and Omphale had at least one son together.

6.147 Callimachus

Asclepius, you have received in full
The payment vowed to you by Aceso
In prayer for his wife Demodice.
You know; but if the fact should slip your mind
And you should play the creditor again,
This votive tablet, hung within your hall,
Commits to bearing testimonial.

6.149 Callimachus

The man who set me here, Euaenetus,
Assures us (for I cannot tell myself)
That I am hung here for a victory,
His own, and I a cockerel made of brass,
And dedicated to the Tyndarids.

97

I trust the son of Phaedrus, he in turn
Being the offspring of Philoxenus.

Placed sequentially in Book 6 of the Anthology, these two poems are by the famous Alexandrian scholar-poet Callimachus from Cyrene in North Africa. He was one of literary epigram's early masters and a great literary polemicist. **Mega biblion, mega kakon**, he famously declared—big book, big bad—and epigram was a perfect exemplar of his new poetics of slenderness. Callimachus' masterwork was his *Aetia*, an impossibly recondite micro-epic (*epyllion*) in four books that explored the foundation-stories of obscure local cults (the Greek adjective **aitios**, 'responsible for', echoes in our (a)etiology). This was the kind of deep digging that the Library of Alexandria made possible.

The Library made literary epigram possible too: for the first time, researchers began visiting the old sanctuaries to catalogue and collect their old inscriptions into reference volumes, and those volumes of legacy media became models for 'inscriptions' that were never meant to be inscribed for real. The first of these two epigrams ironically turns the votive poem into a record of payment in case the god gets greedy and asks for the promised offering a second time. Callimachus sketches in the imaginary scene economically and by implication: we are in a sanctuary of the healing god Asclepius, perhaps his great cult centre of Epidaurus, and Aceso has come to fulfil a vow for the safekeeping of his wife through a life-threatening crisis of health. Disease was one such; childbirth another.

In the second epigram, the inscription 'speaks' when the notional passer-by reads it aloud, in the persona of the dedicated object. There is nothing terribly unusual about that, but

Callimachus makes the bronze cockerel sceptical of its own claims. What after all does a bronze cockerel know about anything, including that it *is* a bronze cockerel? A statue cannot bend to see the inscription on its own base, and cockerels are not big on reading to begin with. The poem does its notional job of identifying the dedicator, dedicatee(s), and gifted object, but it goes out of its way to provoke scepticism about its own scenario.

'The Tyndarids' are Castor and Pollux, twin sons of Leda, the wife of King Tyndareus of Sparta, and brothers to Helen of Troy. They are more commonly called the *Dioscuri* (**5.140**), but as he tells us in another epigram, Callimachus positively despises anything common. Pollux was a famous boxer, so the poem is inviting us to imagine that Euaenetus has triumphed in a boxing-match. Strictly speaking only Castor is a Tyndarid; Pollux's father was Zeus, making the boys only half-brothers despite being twins. Improbable in normal circumstances, but when gods get involved, all bets are off.

Cyrene's other famous export was *silphium*, a famous lost cooking ingredient, known to the Romans as *laser*. Depictions on coins show something fennel-ish. Silphium was found nowhere else and was the city's crucial export. The plant's resin was highly prized as a spice and more besides—it was a basis for medicines and perfumes, and served as both contraceptive and aphrodisiac. Who wouldn't want some? It became harder to find, prices soared, and sometime in the first century AD it went extinct; the Elder Pliny reports that Nero got the very last bit. From time to time silphium is allegedly rediscovered as one or other of the already known types of giant fennel (**6.294**), but nobody has yet found a conclusive match.

6.150 <Callimachus>

Inachus' Isis—in her shrine she stands.
Daughter of Thales, Aeschylis fulfils
The promise of her mother, Eirēne.

The Egyptian goddess Isis became popular across the ancient world. At least as early as Herodotus the Greeks were comfortable finding matches between their familiar gods and those of the cultures they met, even when those gods looked strange. Isis with her human face and healing mission was an easy import compared to, say, the jackal-headed death-god Anubis, and even he made it across: in imperial times one could watch his masked priests dancing in procession through the streets of Rome.

Isis was occasionally identified not with a Greek goddess but with a mythical heroine, Io, daughter of Inachus who founded Argos. Io was said to have spent time in Egypt and to have brought its cult back to Greece. This obscure connection is why Callimachus calls Isis 'Inachian' (**Inakhios**), a patronym he may well have invented for this poem. Both Isis and Io were depicted as horned, in Io's case because Zeus had turned her into a cow (sex with Zeus rarely works out well).

In myth, both Io and Isis were well travelled, and Callimachus does not specify a notional location for the sanctuary in which Aeschylis' statue has been placed. The poem invites us to take a guess, if we want. A cult of Io at Argos is not firmly attested, but that is not to say there was none; there is better evidence for her worship at Antioch. But it is Isis who is named, not Io. Callimachus' own Alexandria had a temple of Isis on the royal island (now sunken) of Antirhodos, and of course there were plenty of others across Egypt.

Isis was worshipped as the loving and determined mother who revived Horus, and surviving spells show that people often appealed to her to protect their own children from disease, or to ensure safe childbirth. The scenario conjured by Callimachus' fictive inscription, and by the imaginary statue it accompanied, is that Eirēne (Irene) had promised the statue to Isis as payment if she kept Aeschylis safe through one or other of these dangers. Now she gratefully fulfils her vow.

6.151 Tymnes

Miccus of Pella hung this booming horn,
The war-god's, in Athena Ilias' shrine:
Etruscan instrument, through which that man
Many a bygone time did bellow out
The siren calls of parley and of war.

6.159 Antipater of Sidon

I am a trumpet, that in former time
Gushed forth the bloody war-song in the fight
And issued too the sweet refrain of peace.
And here I hang, your gift, Pherenicus,
To the Tritonian maid: for I have ceased
From roaring out the bellowed clarion.

Two heralds hang up their horns. These dedicatory epigrams are by poets of the Hellenistic age (conventionally dated 323–32 BC), when the half-dozen rival dynasties founded by the **Diadokhoi**

(Latin *Diadochi*), self-proclaimed Successors to Alexander the Great, warred on each other for generations almost without pause, fielding armies that dwarfed anything seen in the preceding classical age. They got so good at exterminating each other that the leftovers were relatively easy pickings for the new superpower to their west, the Republic of Rome, which took to their advanced technologies of war—siege towers, ballistas, and such—like a duck to water.

By Hellenistic times the cult of Athena Ilias was already ancient. As its name suggests, it was based at Ilium (**9.97**), the city that we call Troy and that generates the title of Homer's *Iliad* (Troy Story). The Cyclic poems that round out Homer's story tell us that Troy was kept safe by an ancient and heaven-sent cult statue of Athena, the Palladium; the Greeks had to sneak it out before the city could fall. The London Palladium is thus a shrine to Athena and her arts. We know from coin finds that from the fourth century BC a 'Confederation of Athena Ilias' celebrated a Panhellenic festival where once, mythic aeons before, swift-footed Achilles had honoured his beloved Patroclus with funeral games. The cult was clearly important. Miccus has travelled from Macedonia, and his trumpet has come even further from its place of manufacture in central western Italy.

Nothing is left of Athena Ilias' sanctuary in any of its iterations. The site's first excavator, Heinrich Schliemann, was a man of heroic convictions who obliterated swathes of stratigraphy (**9.97**) on his way down to a Troy he could reckon fit for Homer. This wealthy businessman and self-taught digger had previously excavated at Mycenae, finding a gold funeral mask that famously inspired him to declare he had 'gazed upon the face of Agamemnon'. Conventional academic wisdom of the day said there had never been a real Troy, but this amateur read translations of classical texts including the *Iliad* and then went and dug where the ancient Greeks had always agreed it had stood, and indeed where it was known that later so-called Troys/Iliums had been built (on top of it, as it turned out) by Greek colonists and Romans too. The latter were attracted as settlers and tourists not just by the sweet location but by nostalgia for the birthplace of their indirect founder, Aeneas, prince of Troy (**7.137**) and an important Homeric hero in his own right as well as ancestor of the Caesars and star of Virgil's *Aeneid*. Schliemann sank his trenches and: hey presto. It was not *exactly* Homer's Troy, because Homer's epics are sagas rather than documentaries, but only a nutter would deny he was in the right place.

Of course, the ancient world attracts nutters (though Greece and Rome have it easy compared to Egypt) and there are amateur controversialists who will tell you the *real* Troy was somewhere else altogether. Finland, for instance, or Cambridge, because doesn't Ely sound like Ilium? I wish I was kidding you about that.

6.171 Anonymous

For you, no other, did the Rhodians,
Sons of a Doric isle, labour an age
To raise a mighty statue—you, the Sun;
It reached towards Olympus, for the time
They stemmed the brazen tidal-wave of siege
And wrought a garland for their fatherland
Out of the war-gear of their enemies.
Not just at sea, but all across their land
They planted the sweet light of liberty,

> Defying the enslaver. Those who spring
> From blood of Heracles can claim the rule
> Of land and sea as their inheritance.

Where my translation has 'siege', the Greek has Enyo, a goddess of war (no relation to Enya) who specializes in the destruction of cities. This anonymous epigram celebrates the Colossus of Rhodes, one of the Seven Wonders of the Ancient World (compare **5.9**, **6.10**), built in 280 BC.

The story went that the bronze shell of this gigantic hollow statue (it will have been built on a wooden framework, like Phidias' giant cult statues of Athena Parthenon at Athens and Zeus at Olympia, **12.65**) was made from the melted-down siege engines left behind by Demetrius Poliorcetes ('Besieger of cities') after his unsuccessful siege of 305–4. By choosing bronze the people of Rhodes—a name that, as on many islands, denotes both the island and its principal **polis**—were making an extravagant assertion of ambition and staying power. Bronze was tempting stuff. An alloy of copper and tin, it was versatile, durable, relatively easy to work, and endlessly recyclable. Ingots became breastplates became coins became naval rams became statues became cooking-pots, in an endless cycle of reuse. We are used to thinking of classical sculpture in terms of marble, but that is only because marble is less valuable once broken down—though it *can* be broken down, and countless ancient statues ended their days burned in kilns to make lime for cement. Marble was a fine material, and rarely cheap unless it was very local (stone was dear to shift), but if expense was no object bronze was the connoisseur's choice. It was also hideously vulnerable to expropriation by warlords in need of armour and coin or just by common thieves.

All of this means that the prized minority of statues in bronze had a much slimmer chance of survival than the majority in stone; in fact we only find examples that were deliberately hidden or accidentally lost (for instance in shipwreck or earthquake) before the next thief or warlord could get to them. So it is no surprise that the Colossus of Rhodes did not last. Too big for its boots, it fell down in an earthquake fifty-odd years later and its bronze went back into circulation as breastplates, cooking-pots, and all the rest. In fact the Seven Wonders of the Ancient World had a dismal survival rate. Phidias' Olympian Zeus, stripped for parts; the Temple of Artemis at Ephesus, destroyed by fire; the Hanging Gardens of Babylon, gone to weeds and legend.

The only Wonder that survives is the Great Pyramid at Giza, hard to get rid of though no longer as shiny as back in the day. Did you know that a Roman woman once carved a poem on it, in memory of her dead brother? Horace had written in and of his own *Odes* (3.30) that 'I have raised a monument more lasting than bronze, and taller than the royal tomb of the pyramids' and Terentia upped the ante by inscribing her take *on* an actual pyramid sometime in the second century AD:

> I've seen the pyramids, my brother dear,
> But you have not: for you I shed a tear
> In sorrow here, for I could do no more,
> And carve my sorrow here to fix in stone
> The record of our loss, so that your name,
> Decimus Gentianus, may endure:
> Comrade in Trajan's triumphs, censor, priest,
> And consul too by thirty; then, no more.

We only have Terentia's poem through a transcription made by a half-literate German pilgrim in the late Middle Ages. Such is the power of entropy (in the form of local quarrying of the pyramids' valuable stone facing) that all trace of it has long vanished.

Did you know that *pyramid* is not an Egyptian word? It is a nickname given to these colossal tombs by visiting Greeks of the classical age. They called them 'pyramids' because they are pyramidal: that is to say, they are shaped like **puramides**, little pointy honey-cakes with a square base (the Greeks loved their sweets). This is not the only jokey name they slapped onto the built mysteries of a civilization they recognized as much older than their own. Picture an obelisk, such as Cleopatra's Needle. Does it make you think of a kebab stick? Well, the Greeks thought it did, and that is what obelisk means. Occasionally in a classical text you will see a word or phrase placed between what look like little swords, †thus†. This means the text makes no sense as it stands and scholars don't know how to fix it. The broken bit has been skewered, or *obelized*.

Coming back round to Colossi, there was later a second famous one at Rome. It was a gigantic statue of Nero, and it stood next to the huge ornamental lake in his Golden House (*Domus Aurea*) palace complex. After his downfall in AD 68 the new Flavian regime remodelled its face to make it a Colossus of the Sun. Right beside it in place of the lake they built a huge new amphitheatre, called by the Romans the Flavian Amphitheatre for the obvious reason. We know it by the later name of Colosseum, and it started being called that not because it was colossal, but because it was *next to the Colossus*. In the early second century the Emperor Hadrian (always a great builder) used elephants to tow that statue a short distance uphill to his new Temple of Venus and Roma, but close by the Colosseum you can still see the stone base on which its towering Neronian namesake originally stood.

6.206 Antipater <of Sidon>

These sandals that were comfy on her feet,
Labour of love of skilful shoemakers,
Bitinna gives; Philaenis brings the net
That tamed her straying hair, dyed in the blooms
Of surging sea; and as for Anticleia,
She gives her fan; the veil that hid her face,
Worked delicately as a spider-web,
Is pretty Heracleia's; and the snake,
Her shapely ankles' golden ornament,
Well coiled, from she who shares her father's name,
Our Aristoteleia. These best friends,
Alike in age, now dedicate their gifts
To Cythereia the Uranian.

6.208 Antipater <of Thessalonica>

The one with sandals is Menecratis;
Phēmonoe it is that brings the cloak,
And Praxo has the cup. That is the shrine
Of Aphrodite, and her statue too.
The work is Aristomachus', of Thrace.
All three are citizens, and courtesans;
But they have chanced to meet the Cyprian
In mellow mood, and now each one of them
Becomes the property of just one man.

Two sets of three girlfriends thank the goddess of love and marriage. The Thessalonian Antipater's poem responds to his Sidonian namesake's model across two centuries. It's no accident that both poems are triads. The Greeks liked threes of things, and the dedicatory poems of the Anthology include, for instance, several variants of offerings by three hunters of the gear they used to catch their three different quarries (beasts, birds, and fish) as they retire from their trade.

Literary epigram began by imitating inscriptions and playing around with their tropes (**6.147–9**), and as early as Callimachus' older contemporary Philetas we find the hunter poems parodied in versions that substitute three call-girls instead. The second poem sits within a whole sequence of similar poems in the Anthology as we have it. It is written as if to caption a painting, a suitable memento for dedication to pagan powers (**6.341**) and Christian ones too. These three friends have found nice men with whom to settle down and make babies; in real life getting out of the game can rarely have been so straightforward, but in epigram it's a familiar cliché. They have been accustomed to being out and about at night (the cloak) and attending symposia (the cup) but now they leave the care of Pandemic (vulgar) Aphrodite, patron of their trade, for that of the Uranian (heavenly) Aphrodite who safeguards marriage. They have earned well in their time, and invested in glamour: Philaenis' hair-net is dyed scarlet with orchil, made from seaweed (**6.24**).

The women of the first poem are younger. Families in classical Greece tended to marry off daughters in their mid-teens to men probably twice their age, a nasty business by modern standards. Heracleia's delicate veil marks the three as respectable: in Athens at least, women from 'good' families routinely went veiled when they were out in public, which in theory ought to have been seldom. Lloyd Llewellyn-Jones has written a book about it by the wonderful title *Aphrodite's Tortoise*.

6.222 Theodoridas

The *scolopendra* with a thousand feet,
That depths of sea stirred by Orion's storm
Cast on the reefs of the Apulians:
The masters of the deep-hulled merchantmen,
Ten oars a side, hung up this giant rib
Of cartilage from off that bristling beast,
Nailed in a temple to divinities.

The giant scolopendra was the largest and most feared sea-monster in the ancient Mediterranean. This piece of one came ashore in storm season. Orion rises in July and sets in November, and was anciently associated with tempests at both times of year: Book 1 of Virgil's *Aeneid* has Orion stir up a sudden storm that drives the refugee Trojans' ships onto reefs off North Africa, just as the storm of Theodoridas' epigram casts the scolopendra onto the reefs of Italy's heel. He was a poet of Syracuse, so Apulia ('Iapygia' in the Greek) was not too far from home.

The Anthology has two poems on the scolopendra—the second, by one of the Antipaters, comes straight afterwards:

This ragged remnant of an ocean beast,
The scolopendra, twice four fathoms long,
Tossed in the surf upon a sandy shore,
All mangled by the reef, Hermōnax found
When he with netsman's art was drawing in
His haul of sea-fish. What he found, he hung
As offering to Ino and her son,
Palaemon—a sea-monster, for sea-gods.

Aelian, a rhetorician of the third century AD, described the scolopendra at length in his essay *On the Nature of Animals*. Here is the passage (13.23) in Scholfield's old Loeb translation of 1958:

> Now in the course of examining and investigating these subjects and what bears upon them, to the utmost limit, with all the zeal that I could command, I have ascertained that the Scolopendra is a sea-monster, and of sea-monsters it is the biggest, and if cast up on the shore no one would have the courage to look at it. And those who are expert in marine matters say that they have seen them floating and that they extend the whole of their head above the sea, exposing hairs of immense length protruding from their nostrils, and that the tail is flat and resembles that of a crayfish. And at times the rest of their body is to be seen floating on the surface, and its bulk is comparable to a full-sized trireme. And they swim with numerous feet in line on either side as though they were rowing themselves (though the expression is somewhat harsh) with thole-pins hung alongside. So those who have experience in these matters say that the surge responds with a gentle murmur, and their statement convinces me.

The giant scolopendra ruled the Mediterranean for centuries. No longer: at some point it went away, to where all the good stories eventually go, but it had a good run. Edmund Spencer (1590) included 'Bright Scolopendraes, arm'd with siluer scales' in *Faerie Queene*'s (1590) catalogue of marine horrors. His contemporary Ulisse Aldrovandi, father of the science of nature, featured it in his *De Cetis* (from the Greek **kētos**, meaning sea-monster, from which we call whales cetacean) on the best classical authority. As a zoological term *Scolopendra* still denotes a sea centipede, much smaller now, but still not to be looked for on the internet by squeamish persons.

6.176 Macedonius the Consul

This dog, and leather wallet, and this spear
With crooked barbs I hereby dedicate
To Pan and to the spirits of the trees.
But I will bring my dog back to the fold,
Alive, unharmed, that I may have my friend
To share my scraps and keep me company.

An offering to the wilderness god Pan (15.21) by a devoutly
Christian poet to whom the old gods are a resonant cultural
memory.

The Greeks were as capable as we are of getting sentimen-
tal about animals, and not just household pets (for which the
Anthology has several touching epitaphs) but also working ani-
mals that had served their owners faithfully. The dog of this epi-
gram is a working dog, the companion of a professional hunter
who has grown too old to give chase; now it will share his thinly
resourced retirement.

Macedonius (5.247) was a Consul (Greek **Hupatos**, High or
Exalted one) at Byzantium under Justinian in the early sixth
century AD; he is one of the poets whose epigrams came into the
Anthology through the Cycle of his younger contemporary and
friend, Agathias. He was especially soppy about animals: here is
the opening of another of his from the same book (6.40):

My pair of oxen, that brought forth the corn:
Accept them in good spirit, Demeter,
Though these are dough; grant the real beasts may live....

Macedonius is nostalgic for a bygone age of pagan simplicity.
Though of course people still farmed much as they always had

done, Macedonius distances his huntsman from the Byzantine here-and-now with an antiquarian word-choice: **sigunos**, the 'spear with crooked barbs'. This is not a regular Greek noun and by choosing it he invokes a particular local setting on long-ago Cyprus. We have it on Aristotle's authority that the word is Cypriot, and it's possible that Aristotle (*Poetics* 3.21) is where Macedonius came across it (though Apollonius of Rhodes also uses it once, to show how clever he is). Here is the passage in Ingram Bywater's translation:

> So that the same word may obviously be at once strange and ordinary, though not in reference to the same people; **sigunos**, for instance, is an ordinary word in Cyprus, and a strange word with us.

Country people often have stubbornly local vocabularies for the tools of their trades. Ask in Ireland what makes a sprong a sprong and not a fork, for instance, and you will open up animated discussion (does a sprong have two tines? three?) in which the 'right' answer depends on a participant's county or even townland of origin. **Sigunos** was so insistently local to Cyprus and unintelligible to Greeks elsewhere that the standard Greek-English dictionary relied on by modern scholars (Liddell-Scott-Jones, LSJ for short) leaves it out. Thanks, LSJ.

You probably do not know, and have no burning desire to know, that Liddell and Scott's *Lexicon* comes in three sizes: a massive one for professional researchers, a tiddler for learners, and an intermediate version for postgraduate students. The trade calls this last one the Middle Liddell. That is classicists' humour for you. Moving swiftly on. . . .

6.224 Theodoridas

You spiral seashell, whisper in my ear—
Who set you here, who was the beachcomber
That took you trophy from the surging sea?
'I am a toy for Nymphs within the cave,
And it was Dionysius set me here,
A gift from holy Cape Pelorias.
He is Prōtarchus' son. The winding strait
Spat me upon the shore, that I might be
A toy for glistening spirits of the cave.'

We do like to be beside the seaside, and so did the Greeks. Their civilization was littoral, spreading along coasts and jumping across narrows such as the gap between Cape Pelorias at the north-eastern tip of Sicily and the southern Italian mainland. In the fertile plains of these western lands they found incomparably better natural resources than in the old homeland (that and population pressure were why they had come) and better lives all round, though they had to fight for what they took (**6.132**). When we call luxuries 'sybaritic' we remember Calabrian Sybaris, one of theirs, but there were simpler pleasures too.

What could more unite us with the ancient Greeks than holding a seashell to our ears and listening to the sea roar within? And what could more divide us, than offering that same shell as a plaything to appease the capricious divinities of the coastal waters? The shore was a numinous place where prodigies were commonplace (**9.14**). It was *liminal*, from the Latin *limen*, a threshold between spaces. In this sparsely populated, chancy, and economically marginal environment, people eked a living by fishing and trapping and placated the gods of in-between; but they also had fun, just like us. Here is a poem (**5.209**) by Posidippus or Asclepiades (Cephalas' sources could not tell him which) about a young woman going for a swim and catching a stroller's eye. As well as being goddess of love, Aphrodite was born from the froth of the sea (**12.84**) and kept an eye on coastal affairs:

> Beside your shoreline, Cytherean-born
> And Paphian, Cleander looked and saw
> Nico who swam amid the gleaming waves,
> And being but a man, he lit on fire
> Inside his mind, and kindled embers dry,
> Seeing the girl all wet. And he himself
> Was shipwrecked, though he walked upon the land,
> While she, who stroked the sea, was welcomed home
> By gentle beaches. Now the same desire
> Drives them to keep each other close at hand;
> The prayers were not in vain, that then he prayed
> Standing alone upon the empty strand.

It is the fate of university lecturers in classical civilization ('class. civ.') to mark many indignant student essays about how the ancient Greeks *oppressed women* because they *feared their power*, and for classical Athens there is truth in that, but classical Athens was always a weird place and young people managed to have some fun when they weren't dying of something dreadful (**5.108**).

6.254 Myrinus

> Statyllius the androgyne was old,
> Worn to a stump by sensuality:
> Passage of time was soon to haul him off

To Hades. Summer dresses, scarlet-dyed;
The wigs of human hair, kept slick with nard;
The haughty slippers from his well-turned feet;
His garderobe of cottons; and his pipes,
That breathed so sweetly for companions
In late-night antics—these he set aside,
Upon the threshold of Priapus' shrine.

Myrinus ('Anointed with sweet oil', **5.113**) was a poet of the *Garland of Philip*, which puts him in the second half of the first century BC or the first half of the next; four of his epigrams make it into the Anthology. In this one a gender-nonconforming entertainer hangs up his party togs. The Greek calls him **androgunos**, androgynous, a mix of man (**anēr, andros**) and woman (**gunē, gunaikos**). This does not make him a Hermaphrodite—that's a Greek word too, you'll be unsurprised to hear—but it does make him difficult to parse. The noun is masculine but Myrinus couples it with a feminine adjective and a feminine word for 'the' (Greek has twenty-four words for 'the' in common use, and a handful extra for best).

Talking of parsing, you'll have noticed that for each of those Greek words I gave you two forms separated by a comma. *Nouns* (the names of things) have *cases*, of which these are examples. **Anēr** and **gunē** are *nominatives*, typically used for the subject of a sentence ('*the man* has the ball'). **Andros** and **gunaikos** are *genitives* (of), often indicating possession ('this is *the man's* ball'). There is also a *dative* (to or for) and in Latin, an *ablative* (with, by, or from). This is one part of Greek and Latin being *inflected* languages (**5.34**), in which the sense of a sentence depends as much on how words end as on the order in which they arrive. Students who are learning ancient Greek or Latin vocabulary must learn the nominative *and* genitive forms of nouns because in one of the *declensions* (families) of nouns, the third declension (there are a total of three in Greek, five in Latin), you can't get from the nominative to all the other cases just by changing the ending—you need to know the genitive as well. Both 'man' and 'woman' are among these bothersome third-declension nouns.

For a change, here is all of the Greek so you can see what one of these things looks like behind the Oz curtain of translation:

τὴν μαλακὴν Παφίης Στατύλλιον ἀνδρόγυνον δρῦν
  ἕλκειν εἰς Ἀίδην ἡνίκ' ἔμελλε χρόνος,
τἀκ κόκκου βαφθέντα καὶ ὑσγίνοιο θέριστρα,
  καὶ τοὺς ναρδολιπεῖς ἀλλοτρίους πλοκάμους,
φαικάδα τ' εὐτάρσοισιν ἐπ' ἀστραγάλοισι γελῶσαν,
  καὶ τὴν γρυτοδόκην κοιτίδα, παμβακίδων,
αὐλούς θ' ἡδὺ πνέοντας ἑταιρείοις ἐνὶ κώμοις,
  δῶρα Πριηπείων θῆκεν ἐπὶ προθύρων.

Aren't the squiggles pretty? **Drus** in the first line means tree, commonly an oak. It is the **dry-** in Dryad, wood-nymph, and is cognate with **doru**, the word for a spear, so called because it is made of wood. The **dru-** stem was proto-Indo-European before it was Greek, and takes a Celtic rather than classical route into the word 'druid'. If we came across someone being called an 'oak' in a book in English we would most naturally take it to imply physical strength and solidity, but this is not the only place where Greeks used it figuratively to mean a man who was old and worn-out, hence 'worn to a stump'.

Statyllius is broken down by being **malakos**, hard to translate because our ideas of gendered behaviour aren't quite theirs. In an erotic context it implies taking a passive role, within the default ancient paradigm that made sex an asymmetric relation of pleasure-taking penetration by the socially more powerful partner(s). 'Malaka!' is still a homophobic slur in modern Greek. I toyed with having the second line end 'bottoming in bed' before deciding it wouldn't sit well with a notional inscriptional context, or with the delicate euphemism of 'the Paphian' for Aphrodite.

This is part of a wider, open question about what sort of tone we decide to read into, and pass on from, Myrinus' original. Typically it has been read as contemptuous satire, but I prefer to see the poet expressing fascination and guarded respect for Statyllius' abilities and determinedly nonconformist life. Line by line, that preference helped shape my choices as a translator, little decisions (hair not 'greasy', but *slick* and conditioned) that add up.

6.283 Anonymous

She used to boast of how she ruled them all,
Those wealthy lovers; never bent a knee
Before the goddess of What Comes Around.
And now for pay she plucks the spindled wool
In meagre measures. Though she took her time,
Athena has despoiled the Cyprian.

6.285 Nicarchus, Apparently

Till recently, Nicarete would toil
In service to Athena at the loom,
Plying the shuttle on the web of yarn.
But then she took her basket and her spools

Out to the street along with all her gear—
Burned them in offering to the Cyprian.
'Be off with you', she said, 'Starvation-wage
Of women who lack courage. All you know
Is how to kill the bloom of being young.'
And she has chosen garlands and the lyre,
That girl, and goes to parties, and enjoys
An enviable life amid good cheer.
'A tenth of what I earn I'll bring to you',
She told the Cyprian; 'Keep me in trade
And I shall render to you what is due.'

The close proximity of these two poems in the Anthology makes it seem as if these two women are swapping lives. In the first, a formerly haughty courtesan has no choice but to exchange the patronage of Aphrodite, goddess of sexual attraction, for that of Athena, patron of weavers. In the second, a woman raised to the loom chucks it in and goes off to be a courtesan instead.

I wonder if Nicarchus' epigram (if it is his—Cephalas was not sure) is intended as a satire on the type of the first. The Anthology has several dedicatory poems in which hetairai give up the tools of their trade, with a particular emphasis on mirrors with which they used to check their makeup but into which they can no longer bear to look. This one, for instance (6.1), is by 'Plato':

My haughty laughter rang through all of Greece;
Young lovers used to swarm outside my door.
I, Laïs, offer to the Paphian
My mirror: what I see in it today,
I hate; what I saw then, is gone away.

The 'goddess of What Comes Around' is Nemesis, retribution personified. The root of her name lies in people getting what they deserve. Various stories were told of her parentage. She was winged and carried a whip or dagger. Nemesis was the divinely ordained consequence of hubris, the aggressive arrogance that makes some people try to take more than their fair share. Pausanias (1.33.2) called her 'the most implacable deity to men of violence'.

The ancient sanctuary of Nemesis at Rhamnous in Attica was well known: later Roman poets wrote of her as 'the maid of Rhamnus' (Catullus) and 'the Rhamnusian' (Ovid). On this peninsula overlooking the narrows between Euboea and the mainland she was worshipped as a daughter of Oceanus, the sea that encircled the world. The temple that Pausanias visited was a replacement for one destroyed probably by the invading Persians in 480/79. It housed a statue of the goddess, the origin of which was wonderfully appropriate to her responsibility and power (the translation is by W. H. S. Jones):

It is thought that the wrath of this goddess fell also upon the foreigners who landed at Marathon. For thinking in their pride that nothing stood in the way of their taking Athens, they were bringing a piece of Parian marble to make a trophy, convinced that their task was already finished.

Of this marble Pheidias made a statue of Nemesis, and on the head of the goddess is a crown with deer and small images of Victory. In her left hand she holds an apple branch, in her right hand a cup on which are wrought Aethiopians. As to the Aethiopians, I could hazard no guess myself, nor could I accept the statement of those who are convinced that the Aethiopians have been carved upon the cup because of the river Ocean. For the Aethiopians, they say, dwell near it, and Ocean is the father of Nemesis.

'They say': the Greeks had a fuzzy notion of where Ethiopia might be (they did not go there). Perhaps it was far to the south in Africa, where the sun darkened the skin (**Aithiops** means burnt-face); or far to the east, as Homer's *Iliad* seemed to imply. It depended on the context of the conversation.

6.293 Leonidas <of Tarentum>

His walking-stick, and yes, *those* little shoes—
These spoils of victory adorn your shrine,
Cyprian queen, taken from Sōchares,
The Cynic; and his grubby oil-flask too,
And tattered wallet that had gone to holes
But used to bulge with wisdom. Nevermore:
For Rhodōn, young and handsome, set them high
Amid the garlands of your vestibule
To mark how he was victor in the chase,
Snaring the elder who had seemed so wise.

This poem blends the conventions of two kinds of epigram, the dedicatory and the erotic, and would be equally at home in Book 5 with the love poems. What is more, it plays with the conventions of more than one type of dedicatory poem. The humble nature of the offerings recalls the many epigrams in which a person retiring from a manual trade hangs up their tools in gratitude to a god for having helped them make a living down the years. The philosopher's rags of this poem, though, are instead characterized as unlikely spoils of victory. Leonidas wrote epigrams (probably for genuine inscription) on just such trophies. Compare 6.131:

These long shields taken from Lucanians,
This row of bridles, and the polished spears
Hung on each side, bereft of horse and man:
To Pallas. Man and horse, black death devours.

The walking stick and the rest are spoils of conquest, but won on the battlefield of love and relationships. Most of Sōchares' gear on that fateful night was the stereotypical scruffy uniform of the Cynic philosopher who professes indifference to society's comforts and pretences. He was imitating the school's founder Diogenes, who famously owned only a cloak, a wallet, a walking stick, and a cup (which eventually he threw away because he could make do by cupping his hands). The incongruity is the smart little shoes or slippers (**blautia**, a rare word). They tell us that Sōchares fell far from his professed faith as a Cynic philosopher when he fell for Rhodōn. Socrates puts on just such shoes in Plato's *Symposium* (174a) to go to a party, in what for him is an unusual effort to look nice. Like Socrates, Sōchares must have worn them to attend a symposium. They are high-end attire, with connotations of eastern luxury, and Leonidas even uses the diminutive form of their name to emphasize what a *darling* pair Sōchares had picked out. So much for his professions of austerity. Even worse, when he came away from the symposium he processed in **kōmos** to stand outside the young man's door and serenade him, publicly declaring his helplessness against Aphrodite's power. Cynics were supposed to take a matter-of-fact attitude to sexual appetite (see note on **5.93**) but Sōchares surrendered to love and social convention alike. Now he has relinquished the apparel of his former philosophical life, and his handsome young boyfriend hangs it up on public display in a temple to Aphrodite, as a trophy celebrating his own success in capturing the lover he wanted.

6.294 Phanias

The walking-stick that kept him on his feet;
The leather tawse and giant fennel-stalk
That lay beside it, and that used to smite
The brows of infants, and the pizzle too,
That flexed so readily and sang so sweet;
The slipper with a single rigid sole;
The skull-cap, from a head devoid of hair.
Gifts for lord Hermes. Callōn set them here,
The keepsakes of a teacher in a school.
His limbs are fettered now by grizzled toil.

6.312 Anyte

You billy-goat, the children have you now
In purple reins, and they have set a bit
Across your shaggy snout, and round the shrine
They train you up to race just like a horse,
So that the god may watch their silly fun.

Another walking stick, and two sides to ancient childhood. Ancient schoolteachers were harsh disciplinarians. A pizzle is a dried bull's penis, now a chewy treat for dogs, formerly a fearsome tawse.

Giant fennel is common around the Mediterranean and rich in mythic associations. When the Prometheus of myth stole fire from the gods to give to humans, he carried it hidden in a giant fennel stalk, smouldering in the dry pith. Dionysus used one as a walking-stick and, wrapped in ivy and topped with a pine-cone, it became the *thyrsus* brandished by his maenads in ecstatic night-time rituals on the mountainside. The yellow-flowered plant grows higher than a man and its stalks are so sturdy that ancient doctors used them to splint broken bones, so they must have made fearsome canes. The name for the plant in Latin, *ferula*, is the root of the verb *ferire*, to hit.

The name of Hermes, herald of the gods, appears as early as the Linear B tablets of the Mycenaean age. Herodotus identifies him with the ibis-headed Thoth of Egypt, who was the scribe of the Egyptian pantheon, and both gods were credited with the invention of writing. His badge of office was the caduceus, a rod with two snakes wound about it; often the caduceus is represented as winged, like the sandals with which he flew through the air on divine errands. Over the centuries it has been used as a symbol of alchemy (the province of 'Hermes Trismegistus', the Thrice-Great); commerce; and latterly medicine. Properly speaking the symbol of medicine should be the rod of Asclepius, the divine healer and father of medicine, but his stick has no wings and only one snake: the caduceus is spiffier.

An anonymous dedication to Artemis on Mount Taygetus, written in Doric dialect (**6.280**), gives us a childhood full of toys, though eventually they had to be left behind for adult responsibility. This girl was Spartan so perhaps enjoyed more liberty than her counterparts in other cities:

> Timareta is soon to wed, and leaves
> Her drums, and lovely ball; the braided net
> That bunched her hair; her dolls as well, for you,
> Limnaean Artemis. She is a girl,
> And you a maiden also, as is right.
> She also leaves the clothing of those dolls.
> So, Leto, hold your hand above this girl.
> The daughter of Timaretus is chaste;
> Chastely preserve her on her sinless way.

6.341 Anonymous

He bridged the fishy span of Bosporus:
Now Mandrocles sets up this souvenir
Of his pontoon-work in our Hera's shrine.
He took a coronet for his reward,
And crowned his Samians with martial fame,
When he fulfilled the will of Darius.

When Darius the Great (550–486 BC) set out to crush the nomadic Scythians in 513 BC he took his great army across the Hellespont on a pontoon bridge built by one Mandrocles, an engineer from the island of Samos. This was before Darius determined on subjugating the Greek city-states. The Great King was good business for lots of Greeks in the first decade of his reign, offering generous pay to sailors and mercenaries as well as artisans. Darius became a byword for worldly power, and Persia, for wealth and luxury. Its young men were gorgeous, too (anonymous, 12.62):

You Persian mothers, you bear children fair;
Truly you do, but fairer than the fair
Is Aribazus in my reckoning.

Once the bridge was done Darius rewarded Mandrocles with enormous wealth, 'tenfold of everything' according to Herodotus in the fourth book of his *Histories* (4.88). The engineer spent some of it commemorating the success of his project. He commissioned a painting of the army crossing the bridge, with Darius looking on, and dedicated it to Hera in her great sanctuary on Samos (legendarily the goddess's birthplace). An unknown poet supplied an inscription in verse. This epigram as well comes to the Anthology through Herodotus.

We know a fair bit about the masterworks of ancient painting from the writings of connoisseurs, notably the Elder and more interesting Pliny, but none of them survive. Paintings are simply too vulnerable to damage and especially to damp except in special circumstances. Our best examples are encaustic portraits on board, bound in Roman times to mummies and excavated from the Fayum in Egypt, where there is no rain to spoil them (compare papyri, **5.9**). Greek in technique but Egyptian in context (mummies!), these haunting images are of ordinary folk done up in their best for whatever afterlife awaited them. Seek them out. Here is an epigram to complement them, written as if to accompany a humble portrait (**6.355**) by the Leonidas who came from Tarentum in southern Italy:

> His mother comes to Bacchus; she is poor,
> And so this portrait of her Micythus
> Is poorly painted, work of her own hand,
> An offering to Bacchus. Please, o Lord,
> Lift up my Micythus; and if the gift
> Is feeble stuff, then know that poverty
> Can only bear such feeble offerings.

Cephalas' book of epigrams that captioned real or imagined paintings (ekphrases, **5.158**) is lost, but many of its poems survive through Planudes and have been corralled by modern scholars in the not-actually ancient 'Book 16' (**13.2**).

BOOK 7

THE EPITAPHS

7.2 Antipater of Sidon

He was Persuasion in a mortal guise,
A mighty voice, a genius who sang
Works that the Muses might have called their own.
This craggy isle of Ios boasts its claim,
For on no other island, only me,
He breathed his sacred last, o wayfarer:
The breath with which he told of Kronos' son
Of will invincible, Olympus too,
And Ajax mighty at the naumachy,
And Hector dragged upon the Trojan plain
By colts of Pharsalus, Achilles' team.
If I am small to hold so great a one,
Consider poor bare Ikos, wherein lies
The husband who claimed Thetis as his prize.

The epics of Homer were foundational to the Greeks' sense of
themselves as a people. They read them in school, performed
them at festivals, and discussed them endlessly. Their influence was
everywhere: Aeschylus said the plots of his tragedies were nothing

A Book of Greek Life: The Ancient World Through Epigram. Gideon Nisbet, Oxford University Press.
© Gideon Nisbet 2026. DOI: 10.1093/oso/9780198994756.003.0004

more than scraps from Homer's heroic feasts. Several cities claimed to be his birthplace, but Ios in the Aegean was the acknowledged site of his death. Tradition said that he encountered some fisher boys there who set him a riddle; maddened that he could not solve it, he starved himself to death (the answer was 'lice'). Like many of the poems that follow, this epitaph by Antipater was not composed for inscription on an actual tomb (Homer had none) but as a demonstration of literary skill and taste, encapsulating what the dead author's legacy meant to those who came after him.

Kronos' son was Zeus, king of the Olympian gods. The theme of the *Iliad* is the wrath of Achilles, and of its dreadful consequences for Greeks and Trojans alike at the siege of Troy; the poem's opening lines make it very clear that all the bloodshed that results from Achilles' anger, culminating in the death and mutilation of the Trojan prince Hector, is as Zeus intends it.

Ajax son of Telamon gets a big hero moment (*aristeia*) in Book 15 of the *Iliad* when he repels a Trojan attempt to destroy the Greek ships. Slightly confusingly there are two Ajaxes in the *Iliad*; this 'Telamonian' Ajax is the one who gets the closeups. Antipater does not need to name the hero buried on Ikos (modern Alonnisos) because his story was so famous: he is Peleus, the mortal father of Achilles. The marriage of Peleus to the sea-nymph Thetis inspired a miniature epic (*epyllion*) by the Roman poet Catullus and became a favourite topic of Baroque art.

7.13 Leonidas, or Some Say Meleager

Young and unwed, a bee among the bards
Who gathered nectar from the Muses' blooms—

127

> ERINNA, she whom Hades snatched away
> To take in marriage. All too apt and true
> Those words she sang, that girl, alive and well:
> 'You are a jealous one, you lord of Hell.'

Hades was the name of the land of the dead and of the god who ruled there. In myth he took Persephone, daughter of the corn-goddess Demeter, in forced marriage; Demeter's search for justice, and the compromise they agreed, explains the agricultural cycle of the year. This poem transfers the motif to the most famous Greek woman poet after Sappho.

Erinna was known for just one poem, the *Distaff*. She composed it in hexameters, the metre of Homer, and it ran to around three hundred lines. A distaff is an implement used in the weaving of wool into cloth; this was women's work, performed within the **oikos**, and frequently singled out in genuine epitaphs as the mark of a 'good' wife or daughter. Weaving was important economically but also to women's social lives and friendships, and the central theme of the *Distaff* was Erinna's relationship with her best friend, a girl called Baucis, who was distanced from her by marriage and soon afterwards died, perhaps in childbirth. According to tradition Erinna was just nineteen when she wrote it, and did not live to see twenty.

Women poets were always a minority in antiquity, and their works did not survive well, at least in part because none of their works ended up on school curricula. For perhaps two thousand years the world knew the *Distaff* only by reputation, which is to say primarily through the literary epitaphs for Erinna transmitted in the Anthology. Then in 1928 the remains of a chunk of it were rediscovered by Italian archaeologists excavating for papyri at Oxyrhynchus in Egypt, and now we can get to know her again, however imperfectly. Their relationship in the surviving fragment (of which I translate only a part) is passionate, with the lyrics of Sappho a clear influence:

> These memories, poor dear Baucis, make me scream
> And groan from deep inside; they are your trace,
> Your footprints in my heart, my lovely girl.
> Those tracks are warm, still; but the thing we shared
> Upon a time is only embers now.
> When we were little girls, we clutched our dolls
> Up in the bedrooms: we were just like brides,
> We had no worries....
> But once in a man's bed, you put away
> All of the things you learned on mother's knee,
> Baucis my dearest: Aphrodite placed
> Within your breast deepest forgetfulness.

7.17 Tullius Laurea

> You friend that passes this Aeolian tomb,
> Do not report I lie among the dead,
> The bard of Mytilene: for this stone
> Was raised by mortal labour. Such works go
> Into oblivion so speedily;
> But if you gauge me for the Muses' sake,
> From each of which great ladies I did take
> A bloom to place within my ennead,
> Then you will see that I escaped the dark
> Of Hades' realm, and there will come no day
> When lyric SAPPHO's name has passed away.

Whether written for actual inscription on a tomb or as a literary exercise, a great many of the Anthology's epitaphs address a passer-by (**hoditēs**) or stranger (**xenos**). English words such as xenophobia and xenomorph carry over this sense of cultural or biological alienation, but **xenos** means both 'stranger' and 'friend'. Giving hospitality to travellers was a bedrock of civilization, warranted by Zeus himself under his title **Xenios** and echoing in the modern Greek for a hotel, **xenodokhia**.

Neither the Greeks nor the Romans buried their dead or interred their ashes within the city walls. Instead tombs lined the roads that led away from town, roads such as the Via Appia in Rome where many such tombs can still be seen today. The author of this poem will have known that particular road well; he was a former slave of the great Roman orator, Marcus Tullius Cicero. 'Laurea' was probably his slave name and suggests he was already prized for his poetic talent: laurel trees were sacred to Apollo, god of the arts. He was fluently bilingual: Pliny the Elder quotes and commends a ten-line epigram he wrote in Latin, in praise of a hot spring at a villa belonging to his former master.

The archaic female lyric poet Sappho of Lesbos (seventh to sixth centuries BC) was a favourite subject for literary epitaphs in which poets praised her as a tenth Muse or female Homer. Scholars at the Library of Alexandria in the Hellenistic age (fourth to third centuries BC) compiled a standard edition of her works in nine books, one for each of the Muses, and it is to this 'ennead' that Laurea (first century BC) has her refer. We have no idea how Sappho arranged her own songs for publication, assuming she ever did.

Sappho's name never did pass away. In Laurea's time her poetry, by now half a millennium old, inspired the love poems of Catullus. Every Greek lover knew her work: in an epigram roughly contemporary with Catullus and Laurea (5.132), Philodemus, an

Epicurean Greek on the Bay of Naples (**5.120**), falls for an uncivi-
lized local girl and resolves not to hold it against her that 'she's
Italian, and called Flora, and can't sing | The songs of Sappho'.
This odd new notion of Sappho as sex music is evident too in this
roughly contemporary epigram in which Meleager breaks up
with a promiscuous girlfriend (**5.175**):

> I know your oath to me is hollow air.
> Here is the clue to your debauchery:
> Your locks, that waft a scent of fresh-dipped myrrh.
> Here is another: puffy, sleep-robbed eyes.
> Look at yourself! The dent of binding thread
> From garlands that you wore about your hair;
> Your tousled ringlets were not long ago
> Ruffled and dirtied, and your every limb
> Totters from drinking undiluted wine.
> Be on your way, girl who was shared around;
> The Sapphic lyre is calling you, that loves
> The drunken revel; calling you as well
> The hand-struck clatter of the castanet.

Later Sappho's books became casualties of attrition, as did so
much of Greek literature, but that only made more space for her
legend to grow in the Renaissance and thereafter. Thanks to pre-
served quotations and especially to modern discoveries on papy-
rus we can now read many fragments of her songs. New fragments
continue to come to light, sometimes stirring up controversy
over provenance and even suspicion of forgery, as was the case
with the probably genuine but definitely dodgy 'P.Sapph.Obbink'
in 2014. This is our controversial source for several new fragments
including the substantial chunk now called the Brothers Poem,
of which you can find translations online.

Sappho in Greek is sometimes written Psappho, with a psi (ps) at the start rather than a sigma (s). Her '-pph-' is two separate and distinctly sounded letters, a pi (p) and a phi (ph).

7.18 Antipater <of Thessalonica>

Judge not a man by stone. This little tomb
Is plain to look at, but it holds within
A great one's bones. You look on ALCMAN here,
The master driver of the Spartan lyre,
Whom the nine Muses reckoned as their own;
And here he lies, a cause for rivalry
For two great nations. Was he Lydian born,
Or native Spartan? Judging it is hard,
So many mothers claiming such a bard.

Alcman was ancient Sparta's greatest poet. When Hellenistic scholars compiled their canon of nine lyric poets to be preserved for future study, his was the first name on the list. The other famous poet of that place and time (though not reckoned important enough to make the Alexandrian shortlist) was Tyrtaeus, whose martial poetry urged his fellow Spartans to defend their city-state in a long and desperate war against the revolting neighbours their grandfathers had enslaved (the 'helots' of Messenia). Historians continue to debate how unusual Sparta was among city-states, but other Greeks certainly noticed big differences (communitarianism, eugenics) and the Spartans actively projected a warrior mystique that we now term the 'Spartan mirage'. In the long run they were not terribly good at war and all but died out. Alcman and Tyrtaeus aside, they were not great makers of art either, and some ancient sources said even those two poets came from elsewhere: Alcman from Sardis in Lydia in what is now Turkey, Tyrtaeus from Athens.

Tyrtaeus' poems were sung in the communal mess-halls to which Spartan men were all assigned, and perhaps also on the battlefield—but Alcman's were 'choral', written to be sung by choruses at public occasions such as festivals. Most of the fragments that survive are from his wedding songs or *partheneia*, from the Greek for an unmarried young woman (**parthenos**), the same root that makes the great temple to the goddess Athena in Athens the Parthenon. These wedding songs were performed by dancing choruses of young unmarried women as they saw off members of their peer group into married adulthood. Spartan girls were great dancers and took lots of physical exercise, wearing practical dresses that left their legs bare and scandalized Greeks from other city-states; the aim was to raise them into healthy mothers who would bear strong soldiers for the state.

Alcman's lyrics adopt the first-person perspective of the girls in these choruses. They have trained hard under older women whom they passionately adore, and they sing and dance in close coordination to celebrate the beauty and physical grace of teammates who are leaving them behind for marriage. The homoeroticism of the lyrics is very like Sappho's and suggests a similar kind of occasion for the performance of many of her own songs. The surviving fragments are translated in Martin West's *Greek Lyric Poetry* (OUP World's Classics).

7.23 Antipater of Sidon

May ivy flourish here, ANACREON,
Thickly in clusters, and the tender blooms
Of purple-dotted meadows also grow
About your place of burial; may springs
Of chalk-white milk burst forth from rocks around,
And sweetly smelling wine from fountains flow,
So that your ashes and your bones may know
Delightful entertainment in your stead,
If there is any joy among the dead.

There are lots of surviving epitaphs for Homer and Sappho—but even more for Anacreon of Teos (sixth century BC), whom the Alexandrians included alongside Sappho and Alcman (7.18) in their canon of the nine great lyric poets. Anacreon's poetry celebrated the pleasures of life and was a great favourite at symposia. From the Hellenistic age onwards a large body of imitative work grew up around his name, a collection we now call the Anacreontea, consisting of drinking-songs composed by fans of his in different times and places and faithful to the spirit of the original. Subsequently the works of the real Anacreon were lost. Fragments of them have now been pieced together from the usual sources (quotations, papyri) but for the longest time, readers of 'Anacreon' were actually reading a mass of anonymous imitations that stood in for him perfectly well.

These Anacreontea had some interesting after-effects, notably the 'Anacreontic Society' of eighteenth-century London. This was a club for aristocratic young fellows who loved wine, women, and song. Anacreon's additional and famous interest in cute young men was quietly dropped from the transmitted bill of fare.

The Society's musical credentials were serious, and it culti-
vated exciting new talents such as Haydn. One of its members
even composed an Anacreontic Song for them all to sing at its
meetings, the first stanza of which runs:

> To Anacreon in Heav'n, where he sat in full glee,
> A few sons of Harmony sent a petition,
> That he their inspirer and patron would be;
> When this answer arriv'd from the jolly old Grecian:
> 'Voice, fiddle, and flute,
> No longer be mute,
> I'll lend you my name and inspire you to boot,
> And besides I'll instruct you, like me, to intwine
> The Myrtle of Venus with Bacchus' Vine.'

The Society had branches elsewhere, including the American
colonies, where the tune to its Anacreontic Song ended up being
borrowed for a new set of lyrics that you are much more likely to
recognize: 'Oh, say, can you see, By the dawn's early light. . . .'

The word that I translate 'thickly in clusters', **tetrakorumbos**,
is what scholars call a *hapax legomenon*, which means to say it is a
one-off, found here and only here in all of surviving ancient lit-
erature. One might imagine that *hapax legomena* are tailor-made
to give dictionary-makers headaches, but long Greek words are
invariably made up of lots of short ones stitched together, so the
problem is not so hard. Sometimes scholars must decide whether
a previously unknown string of letters is a genuine 'hapax' or
something broken in transmission as copyist succeeded copyist
down the centuries, not a real word at all.

The Anthology includes several epigrams that come down
under Anacreon's name (compare **6.135–8**), none of which are by

him, any more the epigrams of Plato are by Plato (**5.78**). Here is one example, **6.134**:

> Our Heliconias, she who holds the wand,
> Xanthippe with her, Glauce too, come down
> From mountain pasture for the choral dance,
> Bring Dionysus ivy for his crown,
> A bunch of grapes, a tubby billy-goat.

7.34 Antipater \<of Sidon\>

> The trumpet-blast of the Pierians,
> The grave and burly smith who hammered out
> Such nimble hymns: PINDAR this dust entombs,
> Whose song, if you should hear it, you would say
> Was moulded by a swarm of honey-bees
> Sent by the Muses to the bedchamber
> That Cadmus shared with lady Harmony.

7.35 Leonidas \<of Tarentum\>

> Agreeable to men from far away,
> Dear to his countrymen, PINDAR lies here,
> Who made the will of sweet-voiced Muses clear.

Pindar (sixth to fifth centuries BC) was from a town in Boeotia called Cynoscephalae or 'Dog-heads'. The place-name is plural, as is for instance **Athēnae**, which is why we call it Athens and not Athen. Like Sappho (**7.17**) and Alcman (**7.18**) he was enlisted among the canonical nine lyric poets of ancient Greece, and the

Spanish rhetorician Quintilian (first century AD) ranked him head and shoulders above the rest. Many stories were told of him, and his tomb at Thebes was still a tourist attraction well into the imperial age (Pausanias 9.23.2). His house there was a landmark too, all the more so after Alexander the Great defeated Thebes: the vindictive but highly educated conqueror demolished the entire city except the poet's home.

Alexander (fourth century BC) was just the kind of ambitious ruler Pindar (7.34) had made his money praising. Antipater is right that Pindar wrote hymns to many gods and goddesses, along with various kinds of lyric for festivals and dances, but he was best known for his *epinicians*, choral songs composed to celebrate victories on the Panhellenic games circuit, literally games for all the Greeks (Hellenes) regardless of where they came from or who was at war with whom. Pindar specialized in the premier venues (Olympia, Nemea, Delphi, Corinth) and the most prestigious events, namely horse and chariot racing. Fielding a race team was ridiculously expensive (5.146), and Pindar's regular clients included super-rich autocrats from grain-rich Sicily to whom his steep fees were a drop in the ocean. Typically he found ways to burnish their reputations by relating them to heroes out of ancient myth. Unusually for ancient lyric, these epinicians kept on being copied out and thereby survive in bulk. They can often be mapped onto known history very precisely thanks to surviving inscriptions from which we can extract lists of who won what, where, and when.

We have met the Anthology's other Antipater, from Thessalonica (5.30), and it has a second Leonidas as well, from Alexandria in Egypt. This Egyptian Leonidas wrote court poetry for the family of

Nero (**9.349**), much as had Crinagoras (**5.108, 5.119**) and Antipater of Thessalonica for the family of Augustus, though unlike them he had not backed a winning horse. He had the peculiar party trick of writing *isopsephic* verse, epigrams in which the tally of the number-values of all the letters in the first line or stanza was exactly the same as that in the second. Leonidas started by equalizing his stanzas, then switched to individual lines, as the following poem tells us (6.328):

> Now one to one is equal in its score,
> Not two to two; for I no longer care
> To have my poems run like marathons.

For how Greek mathematics made letters double as numbers (alpha as one, beta as two, and so on) see **5.126**. Greeks were bizarrely fond of number puzzles, and the fourteenth book of the Anthology has tons of these ancient equivalents of sudoku. They are basically impossible to translate because their sums worked so differently from ours (**14.22**).

'The Pierians' is just another name for the Muses; a Mount Pierus was sacred to them (**7.44**) in Thessaly, a region otherwise best known for witches.

7.38 Diodorus

> Beneath this stone lies ARISTOPHANES,
> That godlike man; and if you seek to know
> Which one, I mean the great comedian,
> Who is himself the tomb wherein is laid
> The ancient comic chorus and its trade.

7.39 Antipater <of Thessalonica>

The tragic diction and the solemn song:
He was the first to build them tower-high
By virtue of his mighty euphony.
Euphorion's son, that AESCHYLUS lies here,
Far from Eleusis' soil, within a grave
That is the pride and joy of Sicily.

These literary epitaphs celebrate the acknowledged masters of Athenian comedy and tragedy.

Little is known about the epigrammatist Diodorus of Tarsus, who shares his name with a much more famous Christian bishop and theologian who came centuries later. One thing we can establish from this poem is what classicists call a *terminus post quem*, 'TPQ' for short, a point in time (*terminus*) after which (*post quem*) something must have happened. By Diodorus' time there must have been two famous dead people called Aristophanes. The comic playwright (fifth to fourth centuries BC) was the first; the second was a textual scholar who lived a couple of hundred years after him. Aristophanes of Byzantium (third to second centuries BC) was especially famed for his critical work on the text of Homer's epics. He was one of many intellectuals drawn to the Library and Museum of Alexandria (**5.10**) by the patronage of the Ptolemies, Egypt's new ruling dynasty, founded by one of Alexander's top generals. The last of their line was Cleopatra, seventh of that name.

This second Aristophanes compiled lexicons of rare old words and made important breakthroughs in the punctuation and accenting of classical texts. All his works are lost. The first

Aristophanes is still ridiculously funny and there are excellent translations by Stephen Halliwell for Oxford World's Classics.

Born in Eleusis in Attica, the home of the famous religious mysteries of Demeter, Aeschylus was a great Athenian patriot. During a long life he witnessed the birth of democracy; fought the Persian invasions of Darius and Xerxes at the three crucial battles of Marathon (490 BC), Salamis (480), and Plataea (479); and wrote and staged dozens of tragic trilogies, each consisting of three tragedies and a satyr-play. He ended his life far from his native Attica, on the island the Greeks called Trinacria (three-cornered). Even in his day talent was mobile, and he had visited Sicily at least once before, at the invitation of Hiero I of Syracuse, restaging his famous *Persians* (one of the mere six or seven of his plays that survive) and composing a new *Women of Etna* that drew on local myth. Driven to seafaring by a shortage of good farmland at home, the Greeks had colonized Sicily and the coastal regions of southern Italy early in their history; the tyrants of Sicily in particular rose to fabulous wealth, in part by victories against rival Phoenician colonies established in the eastern part of the island by Carthage. Hiero's patronage lured other poets too, including Pindar (7.34–5) and Simonides. Aeschylus died there, according to ancient sources, when an eagle dropped a tortoise on his head. The ancients loved a good death story (7.44–5).

One of Aeschylus' sons, named Euphorion for his paternal grandfather, himself became a successful tragedian who defeated his father's rivals Sophocles and Euripides in the Dionysia of 431 BC. *This* Euphorion's works do not survive. Confusingly a third- to second-century BC poet from Chalkis shares his name. *That* Euphorion was a Hellenistic miniaturist whose small-scale epics (*epyllia*), invectives, and epigrams followed the precepts of

Callimachus. His works influenced Catullus and his fellow New Wave (*Neoteric*) poets of the Roman late Republic. We have some fragments of his work and not all of us are in a hurry to get more.

7.44 Anonymous

Your fate was one to weep at, when a pack
Of ravening wolf-hounds had you for their tea,
You who had been the stage's nightingale,
EURIPIDES, sweet-tongued and Athens' pride,
Who mixed the Muses' race with cleverness;
And yet you came to Pella, here entombed,
So that the servant of Pierians
Might dwell as neighbour to Pierians.

7.49 Bianor

The dust of Macedon entombs you here;
And yet before you took this garb of soil
You had been turned to ashes by the fire
Of Zeus's thunderbolt. EURIPIDES,
Three times His heavens struck at you with flame,
To purify your over-curious frame.

Two deaths for Euripides, the last of Athens' three great tragedians. Tradition said he was born on the day of the Battle of Salamis, in which Aeschylus (**7.39**) fought. Like Aeschylus he is said to have died far from home, in his case in the semi-civilized north at the court of Archelaus of Macedon, a remote ancestor of Alexander the Great.

Euripides was as prolific a dramatist as Aeschylus, and far more of his plays come down to us—more in fact than the surviving plays of Aeschylus and Sophocles put together. Euripides was an easier read than either, which helped his works become standard texts in schools in the centuries after his death. As a result, they got copied out a lot. If you look at a list of the surviving plays, for instance on Wikipedia, you will see that a lot of the titles begin with E-, He-, I, and Hi-. Actually there is one more than meet the eye because the Greek title translated as *Suppliants* or *Suppliant Women* is *Hiketides*. This skewing is because one of our main sources is a chunk of a Hellenistic standard edition of all his plays arranged in alphabetical order. To clarify further, there is no Greek letter 'H': a vowel at the start of a word is instead marked with a 'breathing' that is either smooth (unaspirated) or rough (aspirated). Thus for instance Herakles is written **Ēraklēs** with a rough breathing beside the vowel; Elektra as **Ēlektra** with a smooth one.

Greeks enjoyed writing and reading biographies of celebrity authors. As Mary Lefkowitz long ago pointed out, the standard approach was to treat pretty much everything in their published works as at least a potential reflection of things that really happened to them, which led to some very busy life stories indeed (imagine writing, say, a biography of Madonna or Elvis based on every first-person statement in their collected lyrics). There were so many mutually irreconcilable stories about Sappho of Lesbos for instance (**7.17**) that biographers invented a second, completely different Sappho to help carry them.

An interesting death could be made to sum up a celebrity's personality. There was neat logic, for example, in having an infected dog bite kill Diogenes (7.116), the founder of Cynic philosophy, because **Kunikos** means dog-like (Cynics sought to be honest animals and barked at civilized hypocrisy). These endings were often multiple-choice; in another popular version, Diogenes died of holding his breath. At least partly through how Aristophanes (**7.38**) satirized him in comedies, Euripides acquired a reputation for being irreligious, so the poetic epitaphs engineer divine justice to give his story closure. The tradition had legs; Bianor was writing in the age of Augustus (first century BC), roughly four hundred years after Euripides died of whatever.

7.52 Demiurgus

The wreath that crowned the spacious dancing-floor
Of Hellas, and the ruler of the song—
I hold that HESIOD that Ascra bore.

7.54 Mnasalcas

My fatherland was Ascra rich in corn,
And yet my body's bones are laid within
The soil of Minyans, drivers of the horse.
HESIOD, I, whose glory is most great
Among those men that test our quality
Against the touchstone of intelligence.

Two literary epitaphs for Hesiod, born at Ascra in Boeotia and famous, like Homer, for two foundational epic poems composed in hexameter verse. Homer's were heroic; Hesiod's, didactic. *Theogony* taught the Greeks how the world and its gods were made; *Works and Days*, how to live well in it through honest and productive labour, since every farmer needed to know what jobs to do (*Works*) and when to do them (*Days*). Reading *Works and Days* will not make you a great farmer (its advice to plough and sow naked contravenes fundamental modern notions of Health and Safety) but it is much less dry a read than you might think. Another good reason to give Hesiod a go is that his works are much, much shorter than Homer's.

Depending on who one asked, Hesiod was buried at Locris in northern Greece—or at Orchomenos in the Peloponnese, in a place of honour next to Minyas, the legendary founder of the city and of a mysterious pre-Greek 'Minyan' race. Mnasalcas evokes the distant heroic past by making his epigram sound epic: 'rich in corn' (**poulēios**) and 'drivers of the horse' (**plēxippos**) are epithets, a product of pre-literate oral tradition and part of the standard toolkit of Hesiod and Homer alike.

The use of a smooth-surfaced touchstone such as slate to judge the quality of precious metals, and notably gold, was already ancient by the time of the Greeks. Mnasalcas includes it because of an old popular tradition that pitted the two great epic poets against each other, and that finds expression in a peculiar text called the *Contest of Homer and Hesiod*. The anonymous epigram 7.73 celebrates this contest:

> To Heliconian Muses, HESIOD
> Set up this token, when at Chalcis he
> Defeated godlike Homer with his song.

Much to the frustration of the philosopher Plato in his *Republic*, the Greeks ascribed real wisdom to Homer and Hesiod, both of whom had sung at the direction of the Muses, goddesses of memory. But which one was really the better poet, and the better guide to life? According to the *Contest*, much of the surviving version of which is a kind of riff-off of greatest lines, it was Hesiod by a margin because his advice was considered more directly useful in making people better versions of themselves. Homer did not take it well.

7.56 Anonymous

This is a joke that pleased DEMOCRITUS,
And he will tell it quick: 'Did I not say,
"Everything ends up funny"? Even me;
After my boundless wisdom, and the shelves
Of oh so many books, see, I recline
Beneath this tomb. I am my own punchline.'

The philosopher Democritus (fifth to fourth centuries BC) was from Abdera in Thrace, a colony founded by refugees from Teos on the Ionian coast, which had itself been established by Minyans from Orchomenos (**7.54**). The Greeks did get around. Democritus was its most famous citizen. He was one of the Presocratics (**5.93**). Only scattered fragments of their works survive as quotations in later authors, but they seem to have been fascinated by a single question: what might the universe be made of? Was one of the elements—fire, water, air—more fundamental than the rest? If so, what might the consequences be for the stability of the material world that they inhabited?

Democritus influentially theorized that everything was made of tiny 'atoms', the indivisible building-blocks of reality (**atomoi** means 'unsplittables'), all of them adrift in infinite void.

There was nothing else, and certainly no master plan. His pure materialism basically anticipated our own modern scientific universe, though he had no way of testing his ideas through experiment or observation. A century or so later his theory was picked up by Epicurus (fourth to third centuries BC), the founder of Epicureanism.

The anonymous author of this literary epitaph is working with Democritus' ancient reputation as 'the laughing philosopher', who emphasized the value of **euthumia** or 'cheerfulness'. In an essentially random and plotless world, with no prospect of supernatural punishment or reward, one might as well relax and have a nice time.

Epicurus and his followers built their philosophy on this foundation. The message of the atomists was subsequently repackaged for Roman readers by the poet Lucretius (first century BC) in a didactic epic called *De Rerum Natura* (*On the Nature of Things*), but it never really caught on with them. 'Relax and have a nice time' was at odds with the political ambitions and strict traditional values (*mos maiorum*) of the Republican elite; they preferred to inhabit a sensibly organized universe, one they could count on to reward team players and punish deviants. Stoicism gave them a world in which everything was connected, revealing a divine plan in which all good citizens had a part to play.

Ancient atomism was radically materialistic. Take a sniff of the air around you: if you smell anything, that is because you are breathing in atoms of it (that one is true). Look at the book or tablet in your hands: you are able to read it because sheets of atoms are boiling off its surface and hitting you in the eyes (that one probably isn't).

7.69 Julianus

You Cerberus that hurl your dreadful bark
To terrify the dead, you too must fear
At the arrival of this horrid shade:
ARCHILOCHUS has perished. Guard yourself
Against the vicious spirit of his songs,
Iambs spat out from lips of bitter bile.
You learned the mighty power of his cry,
That day a single ferry-crossing bore
Lycambes' brace of daughters to your shore.

(Content warning for suicide.)

Cerberus was the three-headed dog that guarded the entrance to the Underworld. The dead passed over the River Styx into Hades on a ferry paddled by Charon, and bodies were buried with a coin to pay his fee. The poet Julian is unlikely to have believed a word of these ancient stories. He was a Christian, and a powerful man in his own time. The headings that introduce some of his other seventy epigrams tell us that he was an active or former Prefect of Egypt who governed that province for the Emperor Justinian in the sixth century AD.

Julian was highly trained, probably as a lawyer. Like other educated people of the Byzantine age he knew the classical Greek authors well, because they remained fundamental to the educational curriculum. Those authors did not include Archilochus of Paros, an archaic lyric poet of the seventh century BC who had specialized in the iambic metres that were associated with personal abuse and shaming ('invective'). He had a deadly reputation. According to the legend, a fellow-citizen called Lycambes

147

had promised him a daughter in marriage but withdrew the offer; Archilochus went on the offensive with invectives so vile that Lycambes, and/or one or more of his daughters, killed themselves. We are in the realm of cultural myth here, not actual biography: much the same story was told about his fellow iambic poet, Hipponax, with different victims swapped in.

Some surviving fragments include the names of Lycambes and his daughter Neobule and show that Archilochus could be very rude indeed, but clearly he did not just compose invectives. He writes about military expeditions and his experiences in the hoplite phalanx, for instance, and we know his native island revered his memory in later times. But Archilochus for us is an author patched together by modern editors out of small mentions in authors who wrote centuries after his time, and above all from archaeologically recovered fragments of ancient papyrus book-rolls. His works surely did not endure in book form as far as Julian's sixth century AD, which after all was about 1,200 years after Archilochus' own time. Instead he lingered as a mighty reputation, rehashed over and over again in poems such as Julian's.

Here is another such literary epitaph written half a millennium earlier by one of Julian's predecessors, Gaetulicus (7.71):

This seaside tomb is of ARCHILOCHUS,
Who first dipped bitter Muse in viper's bile,
And spattered gentle Helicon in blood.
Lycambes knows: he weeps for his three girls,
Who hanged themselves. Go quietly, traveller,
As you pass by: take care you do not stir
The swarm of wasps that sleep upon this tomb.

7.136 Antipater <of Thessalonica>

The hero PRIAM: small am I, his tomb,
Not in reflection of his qualities,
But I was mounded by his enemies.

7.137 Anonymous

My name was HECTOR. Judge not by this tomb
What kind of man I was, or take my grave
In measure of the foe of all of Greece.
The *Iliad* and Homer are my tomb,
And Greece itself, Achaeans on the run,
And all these things have built my barrow high.
[And if the dust you see on me is small,
It does not shame me: I was mounded here
By hands of Greeks who were my enemies.]

The Anthology has plenty of epitaphs for the heroes of the *Iliad*, especially tragic Ajax but including also Achilles, Patroclus, chatty old Nestor, and even Protesilaus, whose sole fame was that he was the first (**prōtos**) of the Greeks to land at Troy and get himself killed. The *Iliad* is sympathetic in its presentation of the leaders of the opposing side, old Priam the king and his son Hector who leads the Trojans in battle, and the epigrams follow suit.

The Greeks were never in any doubt about where Troy (Ilium) had stood. It was a place of pilgrimage for Alexander the Great, who was said to sleep with a copy of Homer's epic under his pillow; later a Roman colony was founded there (*Ilium Novum*, New Troy) and the site profited as a tourist attraction. Romans were emotionally invested in Troy because of the old story that long ago they had come from there to Italy as refugees. We should remember that Antipater of Thessalonica was an Augustan court poet, and that his contemporary Virgil was burnishing the adventures of the Trojan prince Aeneas, ancestor of the Julian clan, as propaganda for the new regime. The two poets moved in similar circles and are bound to have known each other.

The anonymous second poem runs to six lines, the last two of which (which in my translation become three) are in square brackets. What this means is that that editors have decided that they are spurious—not really part of the original poem at all. There are good reasons for thinking so. The last line is closely derivative of Antipater's, and the poem's thought already wraps up neatly with 'all these things have built my barrow high'. What is more, it appears that whoever added those two lines had not read the *Iliad* carefully or perhaps at all. Achilles, who has spent three-quarters of the poem in a heroic sulk, returns to the fight specifically to kill Hector, in revenge for the slaying of his beloved companion Patroclus. In his superhuman rage (**mēnis**, a word used of no other mortal) he then commits outrages on Hector's corpse until the gods take offence. In the poem's final book they arrange for Priam to visit the Greek camp secretly by night and ransom his son's body for burial, bringing an end to Achilles' wrath. It is thus his own Trojans who bury Hector, in a great mound and with lavish ceremony. The poem's famous last line is: 'That was how they honoured Hector, tamer of horses.'

'. . . And then came an Amazon'—ancient readers who wanted to know what happened next could avail of a sequel that continued the story seamlessly, the *Aethiopis* or 'Ethiopian Epic' attributed to one Arctinus of Miletus. The Amazon of that poem's opening line is Penthesilea, who dies duelling Achilles; so too does Memnon, the Ethiopian ally of Troy for whom the *Aethiopis* is named. Arctinus was also credited with the sequel's sequel, *The Sack of Troy*, in which Achilles dies (that fatal, undipped heel) and Troy burns. These and other poems, generally reckoned then and now to have been composed more recently than the *Iliad*, rounded out the story of the Trojan War from start to finish. We call them the Epic Cycle and take liberties in discussing them because the text is mostly not there to contradict us. Homer's own *Iliad* alludes to the war's grand span and wider contexts but chooses to focus on events occupying just a few weeks close to its end. No wooden horse, no arrow in Achilles' heel, just the slog of a war that seems to have gone on forever.

7.158 Anonymous

On the physician, Marcellus of Sīdē

> This is Marcellus' monument, a man
> Who rose to fame in the physician's art
> And won the highest honour; even gods
> Held him in deep respect. He leaves us books
> That Hadrian, worthiest of our former chiefs,
> Set up in public place in well-built Rome,
> And Antoninus too, the mighty son
> Of Hadrian, that his glory might accrue
> Among the men of ages yet to be,
> By virtue of that eloquence he drew
> From Phoebus lord Apollo when he sang
> The treatments of disease in epic lay,
> Heroically wise, a masterpiece,
> His forty volumes of *Chīronides*.

This anonymous epitaph sets Marcellus' medical expertise on a level with the deeds of legendary heroes. Educated ancient readers would have looked at the Greek behind (for instance) 'fame', 'honour', 'respect', 'worthiest', and 'well built' and instantly recognized the language of the *Odyssey* and *Iliad*. My translation leans into this at the end with 'heroically wise', rendering a Greek word that the dictionary gives as 'prudent, discreet' but that is characteristically Homeric.

Marcellus' home city of Sidē, the ruins of which can still be visited, was a major port on the coast of what is now southern Turkey. His massive *Chironides* joined a long tradition of didactic epic that went back to Hesiod (**7.52, 7.54**) and was still written in hexameters, the metre of Hesiod and Homer alike. This is one good reason for the epitaph to honour him with epic language. The other is that doctoring could itself be heroic. The Greeks who sailed against Troy were themselves accompanied by physicians of divine descent, Machaōn and Podalirius, the mortal sons of Asclepius, a son of Apollo by a mortal mother. Asclepius was himself worshipped as a semi-divine hero and as the patron of healers, most famously at Epidaurus in the Argolid (**5.64**). Marcellus was looking all the way back to the foundation of his profession when he chose to call his epic the *Chironides*, the Sons or Descendants of Chiron. Asclepius had been trained by the centaur Chiron, an expert healer whom Hector called 'the most civilized of all the centaurs' (*Iliad* 11.831) and who later taught Achilles some of what he knew. His name suggests the laying on of hands, sharing a root with our chiropractor and chiromancy (palm-reading).

Marcellus of Sidē has his own entry in the Suda, a late Byzantine biographical encyclopaedia of ancient authors, but his poem had probably not survived to that date; the entry can tell us nothing that is not in this epigram, which makes it look as if its author only knew of Marcellus from the Anthology. Two passages from the *Chironides* do actually survive as citations in other works, though one has been recast into prose. One is descriptively titled 'Remedies for Fishes'; the other, 'On Lycanthropy'. Werewolves were a concern, then as now.

Medicine became semi-scientific in the Greek world after Alexander, notably at Alexandria under the Ptolemies in the early third century BC, when Erasistratus and Herophilus developed methods of dissection. These pioneers were materialists like Democritus (7.56) and approached traditional notions of 'humours' with scepticism. Between them they worked out the differences between veins and arteries, and sensory and motor neurones; the function of the heart as a pump; and the fundamental structure of the brain. Later Christian authors such as Augustine and Tertullian called them vivisectors, and maybe they were.

Doctoring remained a distinctly Greek profession in the Roman world; initially it was met with suspicion, but people liked staying alive. It is generally reckoned that 'set up in public place' must mean reference copies deposited in Rome's excellent public libraries. Hadrian was a great admirer and patron of Greek culture, and was himself an accomplished poet in their language; he composed epigrams for inscription, some of which survive.

7.167 Hecataeus

Call me by my own name: Polyxena,
The wife of Archelaus and the child

Of poor Dēmarete much-suffering;
And I was mother too, at least as long
As I felt childbirth's pains. A deity
Cut off my child at not yet twenty days;
And then I died myself, at eighteen years,
Only just mother, only just a bride,
But run right out of time on every side.

There are many poems for dead mothers and babies in the Anthology. Premodern life was rubbish, and don't let anybody tell you different.

BOOK 9

THE EPIDEICTIC EPIGRAMS

9.7 Julius Polyaenus

Voices in chorus always beg your time,
The fearful ones who pray, the thankful too
Whose prayers you have answered: yet may you,
Zeus of Corcyra's pasture under plough,
Pay close attention to this prayer of mine.
Say it will happen, give me true belief
That I may safe return from exile now
And live at home, at rest from endless grief.

Corcyra is the modern Corfu, the wildlife paradise of Gerald Durrell's *My Family and Other Animals* (1956) and a popular beach destination. Settled in the eighth century BC by Corinth, it had good farmland and was advantageously placed on the sailing route between the ancient city-states and their colonies in southern Italy (**5.169**). The Corcyraeans never got on with their metropolis ('mother city') and allied with Athens against it in 435 BC, starting a phase of hostility that escalated into a full-blown ancient Greek World War.

A Book of Greek Life: The Ancient World Through Epigram. Gideon Nisbet, Oxford University Press.
© Gideon Nisbet 2026. DOI: 10.1093/oso/9780198994756.003.0005

The Peloponnesian War (431–404) has far too many syllables and its history is even more of a mouthful. The Peloponnese, literally the Island of Pelops, is the big chunk of mainland sticking out at the bottom left on the map of Greece and joined to the rest at the Isthmus at Corinth; but the war that is named for it ranged much more widely. In the aftermath of the Persian invasion of 480–479 Athens had recruited hundreds of Aegean city-states into a powerful naval association for mutual defence, headquartered at neutral Delos and called the Delian League, which they then began turning into a tribute-paying empire. Over a half-century allies effectively became subjects and Athens grew ever richer and more powerful. Sparta and Corinth felt threatened, and they were not the only ones. The two sides were fairly evenly matched—Sparta supreme on land, Athens at sea—and they both made mistakes, the silliest being when Athens, a city no bigger than modern Southampton, was talked into invading the whole of Sicily (415–413). So the war dragged on for twenty-seven horrible years (its main historian, Thucydides, died before he could finish writing it all up). In the end the Peloponnesian alliance only won by throwing in with the very same Persians against whom they had made such a big deal of standing at Thermopylae.

Corcyra meanwhile suffered bloody coups and counter-coups as oligarchic and democratic factions fought for its control, which makes an irresistible context for this epigram by Polyaenus. There is just one snag: he was not there. The *Julius* of Polyaenus' name is a giveaway: he lived four centuries or so after Athens surrendered, and his lost poems in praise of Rome's military victories against the Parthians are probably what induced Julius Caesar to award him Roman citizenship and a new first name. He was not even from Corcyra, but from Sardis in what is now Turkey, where he had taught rhetoric. Probably he put in at the island on his way to Italy and it may have given him the idea for the poem.

This poem then is a miniature performance on the page, composed by a professional public speaker. The new fashion in Greek oratory was for *epideictic* rhetoric. This means a *demonstration* or *display* of rhetorical technique, put together not to inform or persuade (the traditional functions of forensic and political oratory) but to have fun and show off. Since the Greeks liked showing off as much as anybody, the Anthology's book of epideictic epigrams is by far its longest.

9.14 Antiphilus of Byzantium

Sailing beneath the maritime lagoon
With furtive oarsmanship, an octopus:
Phaedo descried it, grabbed, and quickly threw
Upon the beach, before it could entwine
His arm in eightfold spiral manacles.
Thrown like a discus, down the creature came
Upon the luckless lodging of a hare,
And bound the cowering coney in its gyre:
The catch turned catcher so, and you, old man,
Have unexpected bounty from each side:
One from the dry, the other from the tide.

9.17 Germanicus Caesar

From highest mountain peak a hare once fell
Into the ocean deep, so mad it was
To dodge the savage biting of a dog;

157

Yet even so it could not get away
From wicked fate. A creature of the sea
Laid hold at once, bereaving it of breath.
Out of the hearth-fire straight into the flame,
The saying goes, and so it was for you:
An unseen power raised you to be feast,
On land or sea, for any doggy beast.

Epideictic rhetoric was not about the real world; its teachers often set their students unlikely and paradoxical topics on which to declaim, and epideictic epigram shares this taste for the bizarre. The genre of epigram had long since taken a pastoral turn, so many of the paradoxes of Book 9 relate to the natural world of countryside and seashore. Greek readers in the early centuries AD knew the score and enjoyed the make-believe, the inventive turns of phrase, and the displays of obscure erudition. 'Coney' here is a specifically Spartan word for hare that will have sent some of them running to their dictionaries (and yes, they had dictionaries); the word I pick apart and render as 'entwine . . . eightfold' is a hapax (**8.23**) that appears nowhere else in surviving literature.

The exact same octopus-hare scenario appears again at 9.227, by Bianor. Elsewhere in the book a goat suckles a wolf (anon. 9.47), a hunting-dog drowns while chasing dolphins (Philip 9.83), a mouse suffocates inside an oyster (Antiphilus 9.86), a traveller is eaten alive by wolves while swimming in the middle of the Nile (anon. 9.252), and an escaped pet parrot teaches the whole jungle to sing 'Hail, Caesar!' (Crinagoras 9.562). How wonderful to have inhabited such a world, however ironically.

The game of make-believe was proudly Greek in its frame of reference, but some of its players were important Romans to whom Achilles and Homer were as culturally foundational as

Aeneas and Virgil. The author of the second poem was a popular military hero who would probably have become Rome's third emperor if he had not died of illness. His hare escapes a dog only to be eaten by a dogfish, the name by which we still call a species of small shark. Germanicus was not the first or the last to make this joke (compare 9.371), but he liked the play on words so much that he wrote a second version of it, preserved alongside it in the Anthology (9.18), this time dragging in Sirius the Dog Star (**6.53**) as well. The popular saying he quotes is the ancient prototype of our 'Out of the frying-pan, into the fire'.

Other Anthology poets lived to claim the throne. We have a poem by the Emperor Trajan (11.418, a joke about a man with a big nose) and several by his adopted heir Hadrian, who was a passionate *Philhellene* (lover of Greek things). As a young man Hadrian went to Athens to finish off his education and then spent a year as its mayor (*archōn*). Before Hadrian, Romans typically went clean-shaven; following his lead and for centuries after, men of education cultivated beards in emulation of Greek philosophers.

Among the rhetorical epigrams of Book 9 are two by Julian, who was briefly Emperor from 361 to 363. The Roman world had become largely Christian under Julian's uncle Constantine (ruled 306–37); Julian wanted to turn back the clock and restore the pagan virtues that had famously made Rome great. He got off to a great start but died under unclear circumstances while campaigning against the Sassanid Persians. Nothing in the known events of his life points towards the topics of his two surviving epigrams: a pipe-organ (9.365), and beer (**9.367**):

Where are you from, so-called Dionysus?
For by the proper Bacchus, I do swear
I do not recognize the look of you;

159

The only Dionysus that I know
Is son of Zeus, and nectar is his breath,
While you smell like a goat. I must suppose
The Celts invented you from ears of corn
Because they had no grapes. If that is so,
You should be called Demetrius instead,
For Demeter, and not Dionysus;
And toasted oats, rather than Thunderer.

Demeter was the corn-goddess, mother of Persephone, and the proper use of her grain was to make bread or gruel: only barbarians drank beer. The last line of my version falls flat because there is a play on words I cannot get across: *Bromios* ('Thunderer'), a cult title of Dionysus, is quite like *bromos*, the Greek for oats.

9.52 Carpyllides

A man who cast for fish upon the shore
With hook and line of finely braided hair
Brought in a hairless catch: a human head
From someone lost at sea. He pitied him,
This disembodied body; with bare hand
He dug a grave, piled up a little tomb.
And as he dug he found a hidden store
Of golden coin. And so we must surmise
That good men's virtue finds at last a prize.

9.56 Philip of Thessalonica

Hebrus of Thrace, its water chained in rime:
The little boy who walked upon its ice

Did not escape, but lost his footing, fell
Into the stream already well in thaw,
Beheaded by the ice. And all below
Was carried off in current; what remained
In open sight demanded burial.
Unlucky woman she, whose baby son
The fire and flow divided for their share;
He seems of both, but nowhere is he there.

Two heads buried or cremated without their irrecoverable bodies. It was vitally important to treat the material remains of the deceased with respect; if the body did not receive the proper rites, the soul could not move on to its afterlife. This is the motive that drives the eponymous heroine of Sophocles' *Antigone* to bury her dead brother Polynices ('Much-quarrelling') even though she knows she will pay with her life: he betrayed his own city, and its new king has ordered that his corpse be left exposed as carrion. As we saw in Book 7, literary poets often took inscriptions from tombs as their models; sometimes they explored the possibilities of how epitaphs might memorialize people who left their loved ones only part of a body, or no body at all. Cenotaphs for sailors were a favourite. Leonidas of Tarentum wrote two such poems, one about a sailor bitten in half by a shark (7.506). Here is the other (7.273), notionally to adorn a cenotaph for a merchant lost in notoriously dangerous shoal waters off the North African coast:

The hard and hasty squall from out the East;
The dark of night; the swell Orion sent
As he descended darkly out of view:
These did for me, Callaeschrus. Off I slipped,
Dead as I cleaved across the Libyan main.
Spun in the sea as food for fish I roam;
'Here lies' is lies. Nobody is at home.

If that reminds you of the drowned Phoenician sailor from Canto IV of T. S. Eliot's *The Wasteland* (1922)—'A current under sea | Picked his bones in whispers'—then that is no accident. There was a flurry of avant-garde literary interest in the poems of the Greek Anthology in the late 1910s and 1920s, inspired by the publication of the Loeb facing-text translation. Virginia Woolf reviewed it glowingly (the Loeb Classical Library milks this for publicity to this day) and Ezra Pound promoted it as a model for the Imagists. In combination with recently published papyrus fragments of Sappho, Paton's translation of the Anthology powered the stripped-back poetics of the arch-Imagist, H.D.

The Hebrus (Maritsa) of Thrace was a famously icy river in a famously chilly region. You can find a variation on Philip's poem by the Roman poet Statyllius Flaccus in the Anthology's book of epitaphs (7.542), which goes to show how arbitrary Cephalas' filing system could be. In Flaccus' version the boy was not walking but ice-skating, and his mother gets her own little speech of mourning at the end. In a macabre twist, Martial has a Latin epigram (4.18) on a Roman boy impaled by an icicle that broke off and fell from a leaky aqueduct just as he was walking underneath. Martial and Philip were roughly contemporaries.

A second epitaph by Carpyllides under the variant name Carphyllides is at 7.260; this and Flaccus' poem are in my World's Classics *Epigrams from the Greek Anthology*.

9.97 Alpheius of Mitylene

Andromache's lament rings in our ears;
We still see Troy destroyed to the last stone,

And Ajax battling, and Hector dragged
Around the circuit of the city wall
Behind the chariot, all through the Muse
Of Homer, bard to whom no fatherland
Can be assigned entirely as his own,
But both our continents in every zone.

9.103 Mundus Munatius

I was the city that was rich in gold
Upon a time, back when I was the home
Of the Atreides of heavenly line,
And I sacked god-built Troy; untouchable,
I was the palace of Greek demigods,
And I lie pasture now for sheep and cows.
Of all my wealth and power have I now
Only the name, while you, fair Ilium,
Are Nemesis' most favoured, since of me,
Mycenae, not one trace remains in view;
While you live on, and are a city too.

Troy in Greek was more often called Ilion (Latinized as Ilium),
which is why Homer's epic about the war there is called the *Iliad*.
These two epigrams gather up the standard things to say about
them if you were an educated person in the early centuries AD.
Pointing out the contrasting fates of conquered and conqueror
was a familiar exercise. For instance, the poem before Munatius'
(9.102) calls Mycenae and Argos 'the abandoned shelter of herds
of wild goats', and the one right after (9.104) tells those same cit-
ies that they 'are pointed out as the dens of softly mooing herds of
cattle'. Cows do indeed moo in ancient Greek, just like in English
(the verb is **mu-kaomai**).

Meanwhile Ilium was celebrated as having survived in two distinct ways: as a heroic past known through Homer (who was always taken to be more or less historical), and as a modern city, Ilium Novum (New Troy), founded by Romans on a site that overlapped with the ancient remains. Citizens of Rome knew Troy as the birthplace of pious Aeneas (**7.137**), the legendary ancestor of Julius Caesar and founder of, if not Rome, at least the place (Lavinia) that founded the place (Alba Longa) that eventually founded it.

Everyone in antiquity knew where Troy was, and in Roman times plenty of people went there as tourists to immerse themselves in Homer country. It was a good place to have a city. Archaeologists distinguish ten layers of occupation before the Romans, starting in the fourth millennium BC. If Homer's Troy was based on any of them, which is a big 'if', then Troy VI and VIIa are the usual suspects, and it was rebuilt at least a couple of times after them before the Romans got there in the early first century BC.

The Greeks and Romans knew and inhabited two continents, Europe and Asia, divided by the Bosporus at Constantinople. They were aware the world was a sphere, knew how big it was (Eratosthenes had calculated Earth's circumference in the third century BC), and were thus able to divide its surface from north to south into mathematically determined bands of latitude. Each of these was called a **klima** ('zone'), literally an 'inclination'. At the heart of 'inclination' and by way of some Latin is the Greek verb **klinō**, to lean, also found in decline and thermocline. You go to a clinic because the doctor needs to see you lying down. **Klima** meanwhile is the archetype of our word 'climate', which has come to mean the characteristic weather of a geographical area.

On Nemesis, see **6.285**.

9.166 Palladas of Alexandria

Women are trouble: Homer shows it clear.
You cannot trust one: be she chaste or whore,
She is destruction. Helen's lust for more
Engendered massacre, while chastity
Was also lethal: see Penelope.
All of the suffering of the *Iliad*
Was for one woman's sake, and *Odyssey*
Needed the pretext of Penelope.

9.167 The Same

Zeus cancelled out the good of gifted fire
By granting us another source of flame,
Our women, and I wish of both the same:
That they had never happened. Fire we know
Will go out soon enough, whereas a wife
Is inextinguishable furnace-glow,
A source of raging blazes all your life.

Palladas did not like women. To judge by his poems he did not like much of anything. He resented his job as a schoolteacher (9.168–75), his wife (9.165–8), and the passing of the old faiths (9.180–3, 528):

Are we not dead and only seem to live,
We pagan men, fallen disastrously
Into a dream we only think is life?
Or do we live, and life itself has died? (10.82)

Even in a single poem he can seem one-note: the repetition in 9.166 is there in the original. Still, he admitted to enjoying a few

165

of the pleasures of modern living—cheesecake (9.395), Roman spiced wine (502). One epigram attributed to him exalts the memory of Hypatia of Alexandria (9.400), the revered philosopher and mathematician who was murdered by a Christian mob years after his time.

Fire was given to humans by Prometheus, who smuggled it out of Olympus (**6.312**) against Zeus' will. The king of the gods did not want the human race getting uppity. He punished Prometheus with everlasting torment, as vividly portrayed in the *Prometheus Bound* ascribed to Aeschylus. Classical scholars refer to that tragedy as the 'P.V.', abbreviating not its original (**Promētheus Desmōtes**) but its Roman title, *Prometheus Vinctus*. We academics are confusing creatures and not even consistent: the usual Latin name of Sophocles' *Oedipus Tyrannus* is *Oedipus Rex*, Oedipus the King, and it is still often called by that name, but nobody goes about saying 'O.R.'

Continuing our Sophoclean detour, the Latin title *Oedipus Rex* is a happy mistranslation of *Oedipus Tyrannus* (which itself is a Latinized form of *Oidipous Turannos*). The original title announces Oedipus (on whose name see **5.126**) as a tyrant, which is to say in Greek terms a man who has raised himself to power over a city through his own efforts. He is insecure about his socially undistinguished origins and worries sometimes what people may be saying behind his back, but is also proud to be a self-made man who solved the Riddle of the Sphinx (**14.64**) and saved Thebes through pure nerve and talent. Except of course (and here is a big spoiler if you have missed the last two and a half thousand years) that he turns out not to be a tyrant at all—he *is* the legitimate king of Thebes, the secret son of the former King Laius whom he unwittingly killed and whose wife he then married without knowing that the attractive older lady was his own mother. Life does throw strange things at you, as the Chorus pretty much remark at the end of the play.

Palladas' numerous epigrams in the Anthology are perhaps now augmented by a papyrus in Yale, P.CtYBR inv. 4000 if you want to be on first-name terms. This battered and unprovenanced fragment of a *codex* is all that remains of an ancient poetry-book copied in Egypt in the third or fourth century AD. The surviving text contains many Egyptian place-names, so its poet was probably local, and *one* of its poems is attributed to Palladas by the Palatine Anthology—or rather, by some unknown person who wrote in the margins of its manuscript. That is a pretty tenuous connection, but Yale have invested a great deal of time, money, talent, and emotion in their wretched artefact and you can perfectly well understand that they would like it to be by someone famous.

Codex (plural *codices*) sounds impressive but simply means a book with a spine, as opposed to a papyrus *book-roll* (scroll). Unless you are reading this as an ebook you are holding a codex in your hands right now. It is a durable format that lets you skip about and dip in with ease. Book-rolls enforced a much more linear reading experience: as with the video cassettes of a vanished age, one scrolled through to the end (from left to right) and then rewound. Also like those cassettes, they were prone to wear and breakage. They were also hard to cite, impossible to index (you can't give page numbers when there are no pages), and physically tricky to wrangle. Nonetheless classical Greeks and Romans preferred the traditional book-roll for literature; they considered the codex a utilitarian format, fit for technical manuals and craftsmen's pattern-books. It moved upmarket with the rise of

Christianity, a religion of the book that needed to navigate its sacred texts constantly and with precision.

9.283 Crinagoras

You Pyrenees and Alps of vasty glen
That look as neighbours on the source of Rhine,
You that bore witness to the thunderbolts
That our Germanicus was issuing
As he hurled lightning in a hard campaign
Against the Celts, and they came crashing down
In countless thousands: Enyo said to War
'By suchlike hands may we increase our store'.

9.291 The Same

Even if Ocean stirred up all his flood,
Even if Germany drinks all the Rhine,
Not even such a blow could hope to break
The strength of Rome, so long as Caesar's hand
Remains to give it confident command.
Just so Zeus' sacred oaks stand rooted strong
Against the winds that bear dry leaves along.

These two Roman poems by Crinagoras (**5.108**) make best sense in reverse order. The Anthology's Loeb translator, William Roger Paton, observed that 9.291 must relate to a serious military setback in Germany. Crinagoras' Rhine-draining Germans are meant to evoke the great army of Xerxes that according to Herodotus drank several rivers dry during their failed invasion of Greece.

The poem must then have been written in response to the Battle of the Teutoburg Forest in AD 9, called the *Clades Variana* or 'Varus Disaster', in which three whole legions were wiped out.

9.283 will have been written years later, when Tiberius' adopted heir Germanicus (**9.17**) returned to Rome as a hero after his campaign of revenge against the German tribes in AD 14–16. Leading a whopping eight legions, he recovered two of the legions' three eagle standards and inflicted a body count high enough to qualify him for a triumph on his return to Rome (and one may wonder if this spurred any feelings for Paton as he translated these poems in the middle of a global conflict).

Crinagoras was by now in his eighties. Forty years before (26/5 BC) he had trekked through the Alps and onward to Spain with Augustus. A poem later in this book (9.516) recounts a surprising fact he learned along the way:

'Each to his trade': beneath the Alpine peaks
The shaggy bandits with their spiky hair
Pursue their larceny and still avoid
The dogs of their pursuers, by this means:
They take a kidney, rub it on themselves
Till every bit of fat is on their skin.
Its pungent odour fools the keen-nosed hounds.
You savants of Liguria, inclined
More to devise the wicked than the good.

Enyo was a goddess of war, perhaps the sister of Ares and bearing some relation also to the junior war-god Enyalius. Appropriately for deities of mayhem the family tree is unclear. Oaks were indeed sacred to Zeus, who was vaguely incarnated as a prophetic oak-tree at his oracular site of Dodona.

9.349 Leonidas of Alexandria

Cotilia's waters—may they spout for you
As you behold your birthday, pouring forth
A store of healing, that the world may see
Yourself a grandfather three times for clear,
Just as it saw you sire three children dear.

9.352 The Same

The Nile makes holiday beside
Your native Tiber's sacred tide,
Because it prayed and offered vow
To keep our Caesar safe, and now
A hundred axes spill the blood
From necks that oxen willing bring
To altar-stones of Zeus the King.

Just like the last pair (**9.283** and **291**), these two poems make time run backwards in their present arrangement. The poet's name tells us that Leonidas of Alexandria came from Egypt. Like Crinagoras before him, he moved to Rome, paid compliments to the imperial family, and received favours in return. He wrote epigrams in praise of Nero's mother, Agrippina (6.329), and of his wife, Poppaea (9.355); then he wrote 9.352, celebrating the murder of Agrippina by soldiers acting on Nero's orders on the probably trumped-up pretext that she had plotted to kill him.

That happened in AD 59. Nero lasted another nine years, then was overthrown. The chaos afterwards is known as the Year of the Four Emperors (AD 68–9). One general after another threw their hat into the ring: Galba, Otho, Vitellius, and finally a tax-collector's son called Vespasian. He had commanded a legion in Claudius' conquest of Britain then governed the province of Africa, and was putting down a major revolt in Judaea when everything fell apart back in Italy. He picked up the pieces and governed sensibly with the help of Titus, his older son and right-hand man on campaign. With captive Jewish labour they built the amphitheatre we now call the Colosseum (see **6.171** for why). After Titus' premature death from illness the throne passed to Vespasian's younger son, Domitian, an allegedly dreadful man who nonetheless ruled peacefully (AD 81–96) for longer than the two of them put together. If you visit Rome today and tour the Palatine hill (from which we get our word 'palace'), most of what you see was built for him.

Leonidas' epigram on the mineral waters of Cotilia sees the poet moving on without regrets. It is a birthday present for Vespasian, expressing the hope that he will live to see his sons make more grandchildren. Cotilia was a spa town near agriculturally wealthy Reate (Rieti) in northern Latium (Lazio), and one may still book in there for sulphurous treatments of a kind for which Italian doctors still write prescriptions. Vespasian's family was from the area and maintained a local connection; several local Roman remains have been optimistically named for them, including a *cosidetto* 'Baths of Titus' which is neither baths nor of Titus.

Leonidas' speciality was isopsephy (**7.35**). The numerical values of all the letters in the first couplet add up to the same total as those of the second. The poem's first word is **Hudata**, 'waters'. The 'h' on the front is not a separate letter but an aspirated pronunciation of the vowel—one of the first things Greek language students learn is the punctuation ('breathing') that marks these. So the actual letters we have are:

U	400
D	4
A	1
T	300
A	1
total	706

And the next word is **soi**, s (200) + o (70) + i (10) . . . and so on. From the singular form of **hudata** come all those English words that have to do with water and go 'hydro'-whatever. The noun is a bit irregular; as in English, the commonest Greek words are the likeliest to get knocked about (**5.16**). Usually it's verbs and often the same ones we have messed up (be, go . . .).

9.457 Anonymous

What Achilles might say if Agamemnon was wounded

> So now you know my man-destroying pride,
> Our Agamemnon, and you know the might
> Of Hector at close quarters. All have died;
> Your jealous spite bore them a wealth of woe,
> And worse than death the grief that you now know.
> As payment for your foolishness you face
> Sore troubles, an intolerable plight,
> Who were the warlike bulwark of our race.

9.478 ANONYMOUS

What Priam might say if Helen gave the Greeks a plan to take Troy
> What splendid gifts you send your fatherland.

9.479 ANONYMOUS

*What Perseus might say after his defeat of the sea-monster, if Andromeda
declined to be his bride*

The cruel bonds that latch you to this rock
Have petrified your heart: so too may now
Medusa's eye turn all your flesh to stone.

A substantial portion of the epideictic epigrams (9.449–81) is
given over to rhetorical 'what-ifs' that give voice to figures from
the legendary past. Teachers of rhetoric in the early centuries AD
routinely had their students compose soliloquies for characters
from the classical literary canon, so these poems are miniature
versifications of a familiar school exercise. Their authors got to
show off their powers of concision and flaunt their classical learn-
ing: in the first poem, for instance, 'worse than death' rounds off
the hexameter line with the Homeric genitive form **polemoio**
rather than the usual **polemou** (on genitives, see **6.254**).

More than half of these poems have to do with the Trojan War
and the events around it, though other myths are represented too:
Perseus and Andromeda (above), Philomela and Procne, Pelops and
Hippodamia. One poem (9.474) puts Helen in Egypt. According to
this rare variant on the myth she was a faithful wife who never left
her husband for Paris of Troy. Instead the gods spirited her away to
remote and mysterious Egypt, and kept her there while the Greeks
and Trojans massacred each other over possession of a phantom
Helen, a lifelike simulacrum (**eidolon**, root of our 'idol') that they
had made. This had been the gods' plan all along.

Euripides adopted this minority report as the basis of his *Helen*,
a tragedy with comic and romantic elements, but it was most

famously associated with the lyric poet who first sang about it. The story goes that Stesichorus (seventh to sixth centuries BC) first composed a conventional song that vilified Helen as a betrayer whose promiscuity caused mass slaughter. The Helen of legend, by now worshipped as a goddess, took offence and struck him blind as punishment. Realizing the error of his ways, Stesichorus composed a second song in which he apologized and took it all back. Instead he told the Egypt story, which removes any blame from Helen for the events of the Trojan War. This song of retraction he called a **palinode** (compare palindrome, a word or sentence that says the same thing when read back-to-front). Helen relented and the poet's sight was restored. Greeks loved such stories about their favourite authors; they are not at all reliable (**7.49**).

9.608 Anonymous

This water is of quality so fine
It birthed our Aphrodite Cythera;
Or else that Cytheraean entered here,
And bathed, and lent the bath her purity.

9.610 Anonymous

This is a very small facility
But its appearance is delectable:
It is a rose amid the shrubberies,
A violet in the basketsful of flowers
That destine for the garland-weaver's stall.

9.611 Anonymous

Within a little bath, great beauty lies,
And sweet Desire belongs to those who bathe
Within a stream that is the slenderest.

The epideictic epigrams include a long run (9.606–40) of poetic advertisements and mottoes for bathhouses. The ones by named authors were collected by Agathias and date securely to the sixth century AD. The anonymous ones, including the three above, were probably slotted in afterwards by someone else but are likely to be of similar date. The named locations place us in the Greek-speaking Eastern half of the empire that survived the fall of Rome and the West: Alexandria, Smyrna, and again and again, Constantinople. Like Rome before it, the capital of the eastern Empire had hundreds of bathing establishments great and small, some run by the state, others as private businesses. The baths were good for socializing and people-watching as well as getting clean; some of them combined with other facilities such as gymnasia for total cultivation of the body beautiful. Greeks had always enjoyed bathing, but the Romans had perfected the technology that made it sublime.

Agathias claimed in his Preface that the poems he collected in this part of his Cycle were a mix of literary imitations and genuine inscriptions:

... All that we graved with pens or had inscribed
Out in the world, on well-wrought statue's base
Or on the many far-flung monuments
That witness to the breadth of human art. ...

Many ancient bathhouses carried inscriptions of this kind: quite a lot of them have been unearthed by archaeologists and transcribed. These three anonymous epigrams may well then have been incised or set in mosaic above the thresholds or in the halls of actual bathing establishments. But inscriptional epigrams could also play with literary tropes, and 9.611 seems to toy with a crucial trope of Callimachean metapoetics, which I admit is a bit of a mouthful. 'Metapoetics' is what happens when poetry discusses and theorizes poetry; when poems tease out their own methods and aims or reflect on the kind of poetry they embody, often through metaphor. His contemporary Asclepiades played with it too (**9.752**). 'Callimachean' refers to Callimachus, the influential early Hellenistic poetry nerd whom we met at **5.146** and **6.147–50**, epigrams that themselves are more or less metapoetic. He knew the Library of Alexandria intimately and took full advantage, rejecting lengthy and bombastic poetry in favour of compression and obscure learning. His favourite metaphor was water, as in this example from later in the Anthology (12.43, excerpted):

> I hate a poem that goes round and round,
> And I derive no pleasure from a road
> That is a thoroughfare for multitudes.
> I am disgusted when I see a boy
> Who passes from one lover to the next,
> Nor do I drink my water from the well;
> I am repelled by all things popular. . . .

Big muddy rivers were out, pure little springs were in. This metaphor was taken up by his successors such as Parthenius (see note on **5.119–20**) and it is hard not to see it echoed here.

9.615

On a bath at Smyrna

> You premises once murky, tell, what man
> Rendered you wealthy in the light of day
> That shines upon your bathers? Who was he
> That found you caked in sooty smut and grime
> And scoured it to expose your radiance?
> The mind of Theodorus, wise in this
> As in all things: how truly did it show,
> Even in this, his heartfelt purity;
> Though city father, steward of its means,
> He never stained his hands with private gain
> From public property. Almighty God,
> Immortal Christ, protect this patriot
> And ward him safe from all calamity.

The bath-house poems were composed for, or behave as if they were composed for, the walls of actual bathing establishments. Archaeologists have found plenty of epigrams just like them still in place, all across the Greek East. They were written to set a mood and persuade customers that they had made chosen the best place, but sometimes grubby realities break through. The piously named Theodorus (God-given) must have been a local official who paid for the refurbishment of these civic baths (location unknown) out of his own pocket. This Christian benefaction is a late echo of the ancient practice of *liturgy*, under which wealthy locals were tapped cover the expenses of municipal works. Agathias himself, the collector of many of these poems, leaves epigrams in which he brags of having titivated a public toilet (9.662):

I was a place detestable to see,
A mud-brick warren. Here the strangers came,
And native folk and boorish countrymen,
To noisily excrete their bowel waste,
Until our city's father intervened.
Agathias transformed me: now I shine,
Who was so ignominious before.

The windows of the bath restored by Theodorus had been caked over with soot leaking from the wood-fired underfloor heating system (*hypocaust*) or from the furnace that heated the water for the warm and hot pools. Sometimes this underperformed, and another poem (9.617) complains that the baths are chilly and draughty. The epigrams sold a dream that often outperformed reality.

9.616

There was a time the Graces bathed herein,
And baby Erōs stole their lovely clothes
And ran away and left them naked here,
Ashamed to leave and be a spectacle.

9.619 Agathias Scholasticus

On another bath in Byzantium

I know now, Cytherea, how you won
When you were in that contest long ago
And rigged the vote of Paris, Priam's son.

For when you dipped your body here within
You found a way to beat the wife of Zeus
Whose bathroom was the streams of Inachus.
It was the bath that won it; doubtless then
Pallas Athena cried 'I am undone
By better waters, not the Paphian'.

Byzantine bathhouses were richly decorated with frescoes and sometimes (more expensively) mosaics, as well as statuary, and the scenes they showed were all classical. Christians paddled among scenes from uninhibited pagan myth, and the three Graces (**Kharites**), spirits of elegance and delight, were omnipresent there in art and text alike. Here is another, by an Agathian poet called Cyrus (**9.623**):

Cypris and all the Graces bathed herein,
Here too her boy of golden archery.
They left a Grace in payment of their fee.

In the first of our epigrams they fall victim to a notoriously common bath-house crime (clothes were stolen to be resold) that conveniently doubles as a way to get them to model nude ('it's classics' was already a pretext). Some of the Anthology's balneary epigrams must have started life as captions to artworks in these bathhouses and this anonymous poem is a likely example.

Aphrodite rivalled the Graces in ubiquity. The baths were an ideal setting to depict her naked and emerging from the waves as she did at her birth (**12.84**). She is alluded to here as Cytherean and Paphian; the classically educated patrons of these baths in the imperial capital do not need her name spelling out. They still read all the Greek classics (it's thanks to copies made there that we have those texts at all) and the scene of the Judgement of Paris, the ancient beauty-contest between Hera, Athena, and Aphrodite that led to the Trojan War, is as real and vital to them in its separate way as are the Annunciation and other key moments of their own religious myth.

9.621 Anonymous

Come all ye members of the fairer sex
Who thirst for sex—which is to say, come all,
And you shall be so fortunate to gain
Beauty more gleaming. She who has a man
Will titillate him; she as yet unwed
Will stir a horde of suitors bearing gifts
To ask her hand; and she who makes her way
By selling favours, find her lovers swarm
Upon her threshold if she bathe herein.

9.625 Macedonius the Consul

Let he who guides my door and notes the time
Of new admissions be of mortal men
Most true and scrupulous, lest any see
One of the Nymphs who plunges in my streams
All naked, or the Cyprian herself
Amid her Graces with their lovely hair,
Even by accident. Who would gainsay
The words of Homer, 'Dangerous are they,
The gods, to witness in the light of day'?

In Christian Byzantium women and men bathed separately. They mostly had in pagan times as well; Greeks and Romans were every bit as proper in their own ways. Segregation might be managed by separate opening times as in Macedonius' poem, or by a bath only catering to one gender, or by physically distinct spaces within the same facility, running off the same boiler but steering men and woman through separate suites of rooms. Writing about one such bathhouse in which the women's baths are shut off just by a door, Paul the Silentiary (9.520) imagines what it might be like to sneak a peek, accepts it won't happen, and consoles himself that 'hope is more honeyed than reality'.

Whether man or woman, to be clean and tidy (a manicure for instance) and smell nice made you sexy, and baths did that. An anonymous poem (9.622) even tells male customers they are spending money to make money:

> If gripped by sweet desire for wedded wife,
> Bathe here, and she will find you handsomer.
> But if your itch inclines to easy girls
> Who work for money, they will take no fee;
> *They* will pay *you*, who took your bath herein.

It's striking to see respectable Christians in what we could legitimately call the early Middle Ages playing at being pagan lovers straight out of Book 5, but Agathias and his generation are among the greatest contributors to our store of erotic epigram. Their lives can't *really* have been one long orgy (awkward for the day job at the palace), but I highly doubt Asclepiades' or Meleager's were either.

9.750 Archias

On cows <incised> on a ring

> Look at the cows and jasper on my hand
> And you will think the former are alive,
> And latter bears green grass to help them thrive.

9.751 Plato the Younger

> This signet is of hyacinth; thereon
> Apollo is, and Daphne. So which one
> Is of more interest to Leto's son?

9.752 Asclepiades, though others say Antipater of Thessalonica

> See, I am Drunkenness personified,
> Carved by a cunning hand on amethyst.
> The topic makes the stone incongruous,
> But I was Cleopatra's property,
> Which makes me pure; and worn by such a queen,
> Even a tipsy goddess can get clean.

There are very few poems in the Anthology about incised gem-stones. These three play upon the interaction between the depicted scene and the stone chosen to carry it. Hyacinth or jacinth, a rare stone, shares its name with a boy famously desired by Apollo, and **9.571** asks the open question of whether 'Leto's son' is pulled more towards the young woman shown in the scene with him or to the namesake of the stone on which the scene is carved. The personification of drunkenness in **9.752** is called **Methē** and is carved upon a ring of amethyst, literally the stone that prevents drunkenness (the **a-** on the front is privative, negating what follows it: compare for instance 'atheist'). The **meth-** root lives on in methylated spirits (meths for short).

'Plato the Younger' could well be the 'Plato' of **5.78**, who is definitely not the famous philosopher. The Cleopatra of Asclepiades' poem will be one of the six Cleopatras who were queens of Egypt before the famous one, but maybe she passed her ring down as an heirloom.

Perhaps the most interesting thing about these three poems is how they hint at the extent of what was lost during the long process of anthologization, from Meleager in the first century BC (or perhaps even earlier) to Cephalas a thousand years later. They do so thanks to a fairly recent papyrus discovery, the 'Milan Posidippus'. This famous papyrus carries a nearly complete book by the early Hellenistic poet, Posidippus of Pella (**5.186**). As one would expect (**Intro p. 4**), its poems are arranged into categories and one such category is **Lithika**, poems inscribed on precious and semi-precious stones. The Milan papyrus makes it clear that this was a major topic for Hellenistic epigram and that Posidippus at least was treating it metapoetically, as Callimachus did the metaphor of water (see note on **9.611**).

Carving a detailed scene on a tiny stone requires much more skill and practice than carving it on something big, and the newly discovered poems are pretty clearly telling us that writing epigram is much the same.

BOOK 10

THE PROTREPTIC EPIGRAMS

10.4 MARCUS ARGENTARIUS

Loose the long hawsers from your ships well moored,
Unfurl your sheets that run so easily
And sail the open sea, you trafficker.
The winter storms have fled; with tender smile
The Zephyr pacifies the white-capped wave;
The doting swallow with its lisping beak
Takes mud and straw to build a marriage-bed,
And flowers now spring up across the land.
Have faith then in Priapus, go your way,
And sail your ship to every port you may.

The epigrams of Book 10 are 'protreptic', which is to say they give common-sense advice on how to live profitably and with virtue. The book is not a laugh a minute but gives a good idea of what the Greeks thought common sense was. Their ideas overlap with ours, and the book records a saying that is still in use: 'There's many a slip 'twixt cup and lip' (10.32). But you will see some differences as well.

A Book of Greek Life: The Ancient World Through Epigram. Gideon Nisbet, Oxford University Press.
© Gideon Nisbet 2026. DOI: 10.1093/oso/9780198994756.003.0006

The book opens with a run of poems (seventeen in all) on the nature-signs that marked the opening of the sailing season. Here is another by Leonidas of Tarentum (AP 10.1):

> Time now to sail. The swallow has arrived
> To gossip to us in the pleasant breeze
> Of Zephyr, and the meadows are in bloom;
> The sea, just now whipped high in jagged squall,
> Has fallen silent. Weigh the anchors then,
> Cast off, you mariner, and make all sail:
> Priapus of the Anchorage so bids
> The merchantman to venture on his way.

Everyone wrote poems like this because everyone wrote poems like this. They may awaken painful memories if you were made to write spring poems as a child in school. Marcus Argentarius comes late to the game and is trying a bit too hard to bring some originality to the material. 'Takes mud and straw to build a marriage-bed' combines two Greek words ('build with mud' and 'made of straw') that nobody else uses. Same for 'with tender smile'—the Greek **praügelōs** is found nowhere else. Marcus probably invented these hapax legomena (**7.23**).

Most poets cared less about breaking new ground. Byzantine poets such as Agathias were still trotting out Leonidas' cliches a hundred years after Marcus' time. To be fair to them the real-world problem had not gone away. Even in good weather travel by ship was chancy (most ancient ships were small) and mariners promised offerings to gods in return for a safe voyage. Most of the Anthology's sailors choose Priapus. Normally we would think of him as a minor god of the farmed countryside, and we get our word 'priapic' from his generous endowment. Statues of Priapus guarded orchards and market-gardens from scrumpers.

His threat of punitive rape was meant to scare off potential thieves, as in this poem by Leonidas of Tarentum, AP 16.236:

> Here on the drystone wall, Dinomenes
> Set me the sleepless watchman of his greens.
> I am Priapus: look upon me, thief;
> See how I strain and jut. All this, you say,
> For a few lettuce' sake? A few, indeed.

There is a collection of mucky Latin epigrams called the *Carmina Priapea*; a Victorian translation by Leonard Smithers and Sir Richard Burton, with notoriously thorough notes, used to be a rare book but can be found easily online.

10.27 Lucian

> Perhaps you will commit your crimes scot-free
> And dodge men's justice, but the gods will see
> Even the thought of criminality.

10.28 The Same

> When men fare well, just watch their lifetime flee;
> When they fare ill, one night's eternity.

10.29 The Same

> It is not Love that wrongs our mortal kind:
> Love's an excuse for wrongs we have in mind.

10.30 The Same

The sweetest favours are the kind
That get paid back immediately;
The ones that dally, call to mind
Not 'favour' but vacuity.

These four conventionally pious poems are transmitted under
the name of 'Lucian'. There was a famous sophist by that name
from Samosata (**5.16**, **6.24**), former capital of the kingdom of
Commagene and strategically placed on a trade route across
the Euphrates in the Roman province of Syria. These days it is in
Turkey (so much is: **5.9**, **6.138**, **7.158** . . .) and beneath the waters of
the Ataturk Dam. The city's name is Persian and Lucian's own first
language was probably Aramaic.

By his own slippery account (in a short speech called *The
Dream*) young Lucian was apprenticed to his uncle, a sculptor, but
ran away when a vision revealed to him that a proper education
in the classics could get him a much nicer life. He perfected his
Greek—not just the **koinē** ('common tongue') Greek of his day
but also, and crucially for his future profession, the Attic Greek of
the fifth and fourth centuries BC (**5.87**). Audiences in the second
and third centuries AD loved to watch their celebrities improvise
speeches in the pure ancient style. It is as if we expected panel-
lists on TV shows to hold forth in flawless Shakespearean—or
as flawless as they could get (Roman-era sophists loved tearing
strips off one another for getting details wrong).

Despite his late start, and while continuing to assert his Syrian
identity with pride, Lucian became the second century's para-
mount speaker and writer of Attic Greek. His style is beautifully

clear and almost everything he wrote is short, which made him an obvious teaching text for schools and universities back when knowledge of classical Greek gatekept elite social privilege. Which is to say, in historical terms, not long ago at all: Oxford and Cambridge only dropped ancient Greek as an entrance requirement *for any subject* (chemistry, whatever) around 1920, after decades of rearguard action.

Putting him into classrooms was a waste of Lucian, who is amazing. He was an early adopter by almost two millennia of science fiction (**5.16**), gonzo journalism, sitcom (**5.32**), and sketch comedy. Lucian of Samosata is among the sharpest and funniest satirists of all time, and these four poems look *wrong* for him. The easy fix is to suggest they were by another Lucian (the name cannot have been so rare), but Book 11 has 'Lucianic' epigrams that are suave and socially mischievous enough to be by Lucian of Samosata, potentially. Shall we then say the Anthology has *two* Lucians? And if two, why not three, or four? These are not rhetorical questions; the Anthology is our only source, it is a broken source, and there is nowhere else we can go to find answers.

10.51 Palladas

Envy beats pity. Pindar has it so.
Men who are muttered at by jealousy
Live brilliant lives, while those cast down by woe
Provoke our pity. I myself would be
Neither too prosperous, nor yet cast down;
The middle way is best, since climbing to the skies
Can summon danger, while the depths below
Invite the cruelty of those who rise.

188

Palladas (**9.166–7**) knew how to have a bad time. His shorter poems would make good anti-motivational posters (10.85):

Death is our herdsman, and he feeds us up
For random slaughter like a pack of swine.

'Our bodies are diseases of our soul', another begins (10.88). Here he is in probably the fourth century AD appealing to the authority of a lyricist eight or nine hundred years before his time. The world was Roman now, and increasingly Christian (which gave him one more thing to moan about), but the canonical nine lyric poets held onto their old cultural prestige even as their readerships dwindled. Pindar had specialized in songs that celebrated the sporting victories of wealthy patrons who paid well, which meant mostly tyrants. His books of Olympic, Pythian, Isthmian, and Nemean Odes (named for the Panhellenic festivals at which his patrons had triumphed) are not much read now and have a reputation for being difficult but he had some good lines. The opening words of *Pythian* 1, 'Water is best', were taken up in the nineteenth century by the Temperance movement.

The 'cruelty' of Palladas' last line is **hubris**, the violence of the proud and powerful who think that natural and human laws are for the little people. In courts of law and common speech alike it was a synonym for acts that were always wrong, notably rape but also other kinds of physical assault motivated by arrogance and sheer nastiness. Its natural answer was **nemesis**, the laying low of the prideful. Nemesis was anthropomorphized (turned into human shape, **5.10**) as a goddess with a famous sanctuary at Rhamnous in Attica. Her cult statue there was carved from a block of marble that Xerxes' Persians had brought with them on their way to destroy Athens and subjugate the whole of Greece.

They had intended the stone for the monument they would erect to celebrate that conquest. That is **hubris** for you, and **nemesis** was lying in wait: they effed around and found out.

Palladas knew the pagan classics intimately: he was a school-teacher (**6.294**), they were his bread and butter. His pessimism is authentically rooted in the sympotic songs of archaic lyric, Semonides and such. But it also reflects the continuing realities of an agrarian world in which a household could be respected, successful, and one bad harvest away from disaster. Fortune, he keeps telling us (10.87 and 97), is a whore—a **pornē**, from which we get our word pornography.

BOOK 12

HOMOEROTIC POEMS ('STRATO'S BOYISH MUSE')

12.39 Anonymous

Nicander's loveliness is all burned out,
And all the bloom has flitted from his skin,
As if we'd dreamed it. Of his winning charms
Nothing remains, not even empty name.
It used to be we reckoned him a god.
Do not, you younglings, think so very high,
As if above mere mortals: you will die,
And first there will be hair upon your thigh.

12.40 Anonymous

My little cloak, good sir—leave it alone;
Look at me rather in the way you would
An old-time cultic statue made of wood,
With only the extremities of stone,
Polished and gleaming. If you seek to know

A Book of Greek Life: The Ancient World Through Epigram. Gideon Nisbet, Oxford University Press.
© Gideon Nisbet 2026. DOI: 10.1093/oso/9780198994756.003.0007

Antiphilus' loveliness laid bare,
Then, so to speak, you'll find the rose-bud grow
Upon the spiny briars of his hair.

The homosocial environment of the symposium made a cult of the beauty and desirability of male adolescence. The Greek lover (**erastēs**, plural **erastai**) looked for particular qualities in the prospective younger boyfriend (**erōmenos**, plural **erōmenoi**) with whom he aspired to enter into a loving relationship. His ideal **erōmenos** was beautiful in body (**kalos**) and noble in soul (**agathos**), a total package (**kaloskagathos**) that also presupposed a family background of similarly high social status to the lover's own. Symposiasts raised their broad, shallow earthenware cups to toast the loveliness of the city's outstanding young men, drinking watered wine that came to table in red-figure pottery adorned with images of similarly lovely youths.

Athenian tableware often added captions to these images, naming the It-boys of the season: 'So-and-so is beautiful.' These so-called '**kalos**-names' can help scholars date a pot to within a year or so, because peak masculine beauty was famously fleeting. Thickening body hair quickly took the sheen off well-turned thighs and bottoms, and the emergence of an adult beard meant the game was over. Alcaeus of Messene (12.29) conceives the possession of beauty as a relay race in which each runner carries the baton for only a brief sprint:

Prōtarchus is so lovely—and says no.
Later it will be yes, but all the while
His hour of loveliness is racing on
To pass the love-torch to another boy.

The Greeks considered these time-limited relationships as trans-actional, a fair exchange of the lover's experience and social skills for the beloved's beauty and youthful energy; but also as passion-ately romantic and the basis of lifelong friendships. Maturing young men such as Prōtarchus would quickly shift roles from **erōmenoi** to **erastai**, chasing boys not much younger than them-selves, as foretold by Strato (**12.16**):

> Please do not hide our love, Philocrates:
> Its guardian spirit needs no further aid
> To trample on my heart. But share with me
> Some little fraction of a cheerful kiss.
> One day you too will beg for favour so,
> From boys whose loveliness you seek to know.

In the meantime, would-be lovers wooed them with gifts and attentions, and encouraged them to be picky but not to take too long over it. The clock, so to speak, was ticking, though ancient clocks did not tick (**5.7**).

I am usually quite a literal translator but my versions of these two poems are on the loose side. In particular, my take on 12.40 lengthily unpacks a single Greek word for an unfamiliar kind of archaic statue, the **xoanon**. The clothed bodies of early images of the gods were often carved from wood, with stone reserved for just the parts of the body left uncovered, namely the hands, feet, and head. The cult image of Athena in the legend of Troy was one such statue (**6.159**). All these cult **xoana** were revered for their antiquity, so the poem sends a strong message of 'hands off', as well as the warning that what lies under the cloak is not worth the candle.

12.49 Meleager

Drink the wine neat, you sufferer in love:
Bacchus the giver of forgetfulness
Will put to sleep the pederastic flame
That burns inside you. Lover, drink it neat
And pour yourself a bucketful of wine
To purge your heart of bastard agony.

12.51 Callimachus

Top up, and toast again 'To Diocles':
The river-father need not keep account
Of ladles that we hallow in his name.
Father of rivers, lovely is that boy;
Too lovely, even; and if any say
He is unlovely, then let only me
Know and enjoy the loveliness I see.

The point of the symposium was to drink together. The clue is in the name, the **syn-** bit of which, smoothed to **sym-** by the 'p' that follows, indicates togetherness and sharing. A synthesis puts things together, synonyms are names for the same thing, and to feel sympathy is to enter into commonality with another person's experience, however painful (Greek **pathos**, which ends up in our pathology, psychopath, and pathetic fallacy). Guests at any such party (*symposiasts*) expected to get tipsy, and there was social pressure not to kill the mood by abstaining: everyone knew that drinking together let friends tell each other what they needed to hear (**5.136**). But the dangers of losing track and getting too drunk were notorious. which is why each symposium had a designated master of ceremonies, a *symposiarch* (**5.137**), whose job was to pace things sensibly, ration the strength and number of drinks taken, and compère the entertainment.

That was the decorous ideal; the reality must often have been messier. In the first century AD, the Greek pundit Plutarch (who deserves to be much better known) wrote reams of *Sympotic Questions* in which he frets at length about party etiquette. Plutarch diagnoses many ways in which one can end up making a scene and losing friends, and alcohol is at the root of most of them. The most famous symposium of all is a literary one, Plato's *Symposium*, the participants in which have decided they will compete in praise of love after dinner (*deipnon*) rather than drinking and playing party games as usual. This beautifully written and funny dialogue is one of Plato's most celebrated works and a foundational text for ideas about sexuality, ancient and modern alike—but its participants only agree to skip the wine and frolics because some of them are still hung over from the night before.

Only barbarians drank wine neat, which later made Romans barbarians of a peculiar, world-conquering kind. Rome's great families were as heavily into self-control as their Greek equivalents. They also had a fringe culture of heroic boozing that was alien to the classical Greek experience, and of which Marc Antony was a great example; he could appeal to Hellenistic models, in particular the court of Alexander the Great, but Alexander's Macedon had always been a half-barbarous outlier. Meleager's prescription places the lovesick man beyond normal civilized existence, in an extremity of despair from which temporary oblivion is the only release.

Callimachus' distraught lover appoints the 'Father of Rivers' as his *symposiarch*. This is the Acheloüs, the greatest river in all of mainland Greece. All rivers were divinities, the reclining figures of whom were great material for sculptors with an awkward corner to fill in a temple pediment. Callimachus himself worked in the Library and Museum founded by the Ptolemies at Alexandria in Egypt; he may never have seen the Acheloüs for himself, and if there was a myth in which the river-god was besotted with a boy, it is not otherwise attested. Callimachus would be the last person to tell us about it plainly: his own great love was the new information age (he invented library cataloguing) and the access it opened up to obscure sources about which he could write obscurer poetry. Why does he mention Acheloüs? Why indeed? I have no notion why.

12.64 Alcaeus <of Messene>

Master of Pisa, Zeus, I pray you crown
Peithēnor, who is Cypris' second son,
    Hard under Cronos' mount. I also pray
You not become an eagle once again
And snatch him up and carry him away
    To pour you cups of wine, and take the place
Of that fair Trojan lad. If on a time
I pleased by sending you some Muse-made toy,
    Pray give assent to unity of mind
Between a poet and a godlike boy.

12.65 Meleager

If Zeus is still the fellow who once stole
And carried off the prime of Ganymede,
Well, I shall hide Myiscus in my heart
In case the god should steal a march on me
And throw his wings around the lovely boy.

Several epigrams in Book 12 invoke the myth of Ganymede (**5.65**), a handsome young Trojan prince with whom Zeus famously fell in love. To the Greeks he was *Ganumēdēs*; the Romans knew him as *Catamītēs*, which is the origin of the archaic English 'catamite'. Turning himself into an eagle, the king of the birds, Zeus snatched up the boy to serve on Olympus as his immortal cupbearer—and in sources after Homer, cupbearer-with-benefits. Their relationship became a great pretext for lovers of boys. If even the king of the gods was powerless against male beauty, how could mere humans hope to resist its power?

Alcaeus further excuses his own susceptibility by describing young Peithēnōr (whose name means 'man-persuader') as a younger brother to Erōs (**5.10**), the winged son of Aphrodite against whose arrows of desire no man or god is safe. He prays that the young man may be victorious at the Olympic Games, in the shadow of the low, wooded Hill of Kronos, and that the two may then be united in a loving relationship. That Greek athletes exercised and competed in the nude doubtless enhances the fervour of his prayer. The reader is probably meant to imagine Peithēnōr as competing for the prize in boxing or wrestling. Compare the anonymous epigram 12.123:

When Menecharmus, son of Anticles,
Was named the victor in his boxing-match,
I crowned him with ten ribbons of soft wool,
And three times kissed the blood that streamed his face:
To me it was more honey-sweet than myrrh.

The great temple to Zeus at Olympia housed a huge, gold-and-ivory (*chryselephantine*) statue of the god by Phidias that was acknowledged as one of the Seven Wonders of the World. Alcaeus reckons that since Zeus is both the divine patron of the games and a connoisseur of male beauty, he is bound to have his eye on Peithēnōr already; if he does not stand in the poet's own way it can only be because he himself is an appreciative reader of Alcaeus' own erotic epigrams, which speak to anticipations and frustrations he knows all too well.

If Peithēnōr is victorious, he will be crowned with a garland of olive leaves. There were several Panhellenic athletic festivals (**7.35**), each with its own characteristic wreath. At Nemea, for instance, where Heracles had defeated the Nemean Lion as his first Labour, winners were garlanded with wild celery; at the Pythians the crown was of laurel, the plant sacred to Delphi's patron god, Apollo.

Meleager's passion for Myiscus, his 'Little mouse', continues at **12.106** and **110**.

12.71 Callimachus

Cleonicus of Thessaly. Poor man!
Poor man, I swear upon the piercing sun
I did not know you. Where then have you been?
You are just skin and bone. Has my bad luck

Rubbed off on you, and have you met a fate
You cannot stomach? This at least I knew:
Euxitheus had got his claws in you,
And you return to me more sore than wise,
With that boy's beauty brimming both your eyes.

12.74 Meleager

If anything should happen to me, friend—
Because, you see, the better part of me
Was tossed into the fire of pretty boys
And lies there as an ember in the glow—
Then, Cleobulus, I beseech of you,
Make the urn tipsy with unwatered wine
Before you bury it, and add the line,
'A gift from Erōs to the world below'.

Everyone knew that love hurt (**5.10**), especially when it was unre-quited. In a famous passage of lyric verse preserved by quota-tion in a treatise attributed to Longinus, *On the Sublime*, Sappho describes being close to a beautiful young woman who is some-one else:

> … It makes my heart shudder in my chest, because when I am with
> you even for a moment I can't get words out—it's like my tongue is
> broken, and all at once a tingling fire runs over my skin, and my
> eyes can't see a single thing, and there's a drumming in my ears, I
> break out in a cold sweat, I'm shaking all over and can't stop it, I'm
> paler than grass, and I feel like I've pretty much died. …

The Hellenistic poet Apollonius of Rhodes had Sappho's famous
description in mind when he wrote his epic of the voyage of the

Argo to fetch the Golden Fleece. Jason's destination was barbarous Colchis on the Black Sea, a region that terrified Greek mariners; they euphemistically called it the Euxine (**Euxeinos**), literally the Friendly Sea, much as one might address a huge and snarling hound as 'Nice doggie!' in the hope of surviving the encounter. Jason's most heroic asset is his good looks. The daughter of the hostile local king falls in love with him at first sight; he takes advantage of her infatuation to achieve his mission and thereby sets the scene for a famous tragedy by Euripides (Apollonius could count on his readers having done it in school). Her name is Medea. Here she is in the World's Classics translation by Richard Hunter:

> All the cares that the Loves stir up tossed about in her spirit. Everything still danced right before her eyes—how he looked, the clothes he wore. . . . As she pondered she thought that there could never have been another such man. In her ears rang his voice and the honeyed words he spoke. She feared for him. . . . Whenever longing gripped her, shame kept her inside; when she was held back by shame, reckless desire pushed her on.

When poets such as Callimachus and Meleager started writing erotic epigrams, they took on a voice and point of view that was also being used to describe how women felt about falling in love.

12.84 Meleager

My friends, I'm sending out an SOS:
No sooner do I step upon the shore,
My maiden voyage only just complete,

Than pirate Erōs takes me under tow,
Seeing as how he brandishes his torch
And turns my head to see a lovely boy
And want him badly. Step by step I go,
Each in his footstep, and in empty air
I plunder sweetened kisses from the lips
Of a sweet phantom cast in fantasy.
Have I escaped the unrelenting sea
Only to reach dry land and so succumb
Under a flood less merciful by far,
The surge and billow of the Cyprian?

Aphrodite was born from the foam of the sea (**aphros**) and her
great sanctuary at Paphos on Cyprus marked where she had first
come ashore, so it made sense to think of her business as mari-
time. Compare the *Satisfaction* and *Bachelor's Delight* of **5.44**, or this
variant by Hedylus ('or some say Asclepiades'), **5.161**:

Euphro and Thaïs and Boidion,
The oldest girls that Diomedes ran,
Bulk carriers with twenty oars a side:
Each has in turn cast overboard a man—
Agis and Cleophon, Antagoras—
Whom they first stripped, and left in worse estate
Than shipwrecked mariners. And therefore flee
These ships, and Aphrodite's piracy:
Sirens have nothing on their enmity.

Meleager pursues a maddening vision 'stamped' or 'moulded' in
the air; the Greek verb is **tupō** and lies behind English words such
as typography (writing by stamping an impression), stereotype,
and typical. Many ancient readers will have read this in the light
of Epicurean philosophy (**7.56**, and compare **12.106**) that posited

sense-perception was atomic. During Meleager's lifetime and far to the west a Roman, Lucretius, was popularizing Epicurus' ideas in Latin and wrote memorably about how these invasive atoms wreck people's emotional equilibrium. He made a point of combining his observations on sense-perception and sexual obsession in the same volume of his six-book didactic epic *On the Nature of Things* (tr. Ronald Melville for World's Classics):

> . . . . Ah, cursed images!
> Flee them you must and all the food of love
> Reject, and turn the mind away, and eject
> The pent-up fluid into other bodies,
> And let it go. . . .
>
> And by avoiding love you need not miss
> The fruits that Venus offers, but instead
> You may take the goods without the penalty.
> For sure from this a purer pleasure comes
> To the healthy than to the lovesick.

12.93 Rhianus

> Boys are a labyrinth without a thread:
> It matters not which way you cast your eye,
> You find it caught in birdlime mistletoe.
> One path, and Theodorus steers your gaze
> Toward the luscious acme of his frame,
> His body's unplucked bloom; another way,
> The golden countenance of Philocles:
> He is not tall, and yet a heavenly grace
> Has blossomed in him. If again you turn

Towards Leptinus, you will freeze in place
As if confined in steely manacles,
So fierce a flame he kindles in his eyes,
To burn you up from scalp to fingertips.
Blessings upon you, all you lovely boys:
May you attain the peak of youthful prime
And wear grey locks in some far later time.

Rhianus came from Crete, at the end of the third century BC. According to the Suda he began as a slave but acquired a literary education and became a notable author of epics about historical wars. He also edited the text of Homer and wrote epigrams, often about pretty boys. A number of these survive.

The labyrinth and thread allude to the myth in which Theseus must navigate the maze at Knossos and kill King Minos' pet monster, the Minotaur; the birdlime, to the real-life and time-honoured practice of supplementing a peasant diet by trapping small birds such as thrushes (delicious grilled). The traditional way of making it is to crush mistletoe berries to a pulp.

Meleager later produced his own catalogue of boys in loose imitation of Rhianus. His version is naughtier (**12.95**):

If the Desires are fond, friend Philocles,
And sweetly-breathing Peitho is your friend,
And Graces who anthologize the fair,
May Diodorus in your arms entwine;
Sweet Dorotheus stand and sing for you;
Callicrates recline upon your knee;
May Dio take in hand your well-aimed horn
And warm it up, and then Uliades
Give it a scalping; Philip, give sweet kiss,
And Thēro gossip, while you reach beneath

Eudemus' gown and give his breast a squeeze.
O lucky man, if god supplies such joys,
You'll mix a Roman salad out of boys.

We do not know exactly what Greeks thought went into a 'Roman salad' but clearly they reckoned on it containing plenty of tasty bits and pieces. Romans liked their vegetables flavoured with spices (cumin, coriander, pepper, celery seed) or cut with powerful herbs (lovage, rue). The cookery-book of Apicius gives a recipe (4.5.1) for a frittata-style antipasto centrepiece that combines leeks, beets, celery, onions, mallow leaves, snails, chicken giblets, meatballs, sliced sausage, meat from small birds (caught with birdlime as above), damsons, and more. This is probably the kind of thing Meleager had in mind, if not in detail then in its more-is-more attitude.

Did you know that damsons are called damsons because they came from Damascus? Well, now you do. And pheasants are called pheasants because they came from Phasis on the Black Sea, a barbarous territory that had been home to the legendary Medea (**12.71**).

12.106 Meleager

I know one beauty, and in this I know
All beauty, and my ever-roaming eye
Can only see Myiscus; I am blind
For any other; he is everything
In my imagination. Do eyes see
Merely to curry favour with the soul?
If so, they are accomplished in their role.

12.110 The Same

Sweet loveliness has flashed across the sky.
See how he shoots the lightnings from his eyes:
Has then Desire revealed a boy who knows
To conquer us and wield the thunderbolt?
Myiscus dear, you bring the Graces' gleam
To mortal men: among us may you shine,
And, though a firebrand, be a friend of mine.

Desire in ancient epigram enters through the eyes. If one accepted the radical atomism of Epicurus (**7.56**) then the eyes were an obvious point of vulnerability: atoms from a beautiful person could enter through them and go straight into the brain. So when Myiscus 'shoots the lightnings from his eyes' there is more going on than lovely glances, though those too. It's a recurring concern for Meleager; compare **12.60**:

If I see Therōn, I see everything;
But if I see the whole world, and not he,
Then there is nothing in the world I see.

Smitten though he is by the beauty of these godlike boys, Meleager is an old-fashioned gentleman who wants more than just to satisfy sexual and romantic longing. He hopes for a connection that endures beyond the necessarily brief transactional relationship of **paiderastia** and matures into lifelong friendship, **philia**.

Myiscus is the subject of thirteen of Meleager's epigrams, one more than Zenophila gets and only four less than the Heliodora whom romantic critics of the nineteenth and early twentieth centuries wished to install as the great love of Meleager's life. He had no place in epigram's modern public story, such as it was, until John Addington Symonds (**5.65**) upset the applecart with *Studies of the Greek Poets* in 1873. Symonds' heavily subtextual treatment of epigram was an early and barely veiled claim for gay rights, published to a mass readership, and sexually conservative critics of antiquity spent the next half-century and more trying to herd his bisexual Meleager back into the closet, mumbling the whole time. They coped with Myiscus by assigning all of Meleager's homoerotic poems to a phase of hands-above-the-waist experimentation during the poet's university years (I am not making any of this up), after which they decided he must have moved on, grown a pair, and sown some wild oats with Zenophila and others before setting his heart on his perfect lady.

The convenient fiction arose that the poems about Myiscus and other boys had formed Meleager's first book, a work of juvenilia written as a silly young person: doubtless he was embarrassed to recall it once he had grown into common sense. However, the critics never came out and said all this in so many words, because to name the thing was to admit its possibility and perhaps to plant ideas in the head of some modern silly young person; all they could safely do was mumble against 'that odious passion of the Greeks, which among us it is a shame even to mention' (Chalmer's *General Biographical Dictionary*, many such instances).

Meleager dedicated his whole *Garland* to Diocles (**5.147**), one of his gorgeous young men, but mainstream Victorian and Edwardian critics were not going to tell you that; outside gay subculture, epigram's sexual fluidity stayed a trade secret till the 1960s. We come back to the Diocles poem at this book's close.

BOOK 13

POLYMETRIC POEMS

13.2 Phaedimus

Iambic trimeters

> Herald of Zeus, Callistratus set here
> An image of a friend of his own age
> Who looks just like you, as your offering.
> He is from Cephissia, this young man.
> Enjoy it, Lord, and so keep safe from harm
> Apollodorus' son and fatherland.

13.4 Anacreon

Tetrameter

> Oh, Alcimus, Aristocles' boy,
> I grieve for you, the foremost of my friends,
> Who made an end of youthful manliness
> Defending fatherland from slavery.

A Book of Greek Life: The Ancient World Through Epigram. Gideon Nisbet, Oxford University Press. © Gideon Nisbet 2026. DOI: 10.1093/oso/9780198994756.003.0008

13.6 Phalaecus

Hendecasyllabic trimeter, so called

This image of extraordinary kind,
Portraying a comedian all wreathed
In ivy garlands for the festal hymn
To Dionysus: I erected it,
That it might stand above our Lycon's grave,
Rising as tall as one time did his fame:
Reminding us of what great fun he was,
Reclining on a couch and drinking wine.
This offering will let the future know,
And offer proof that he appeared just so.

Greeks did not make their poems rhyme, but they always made them scan. The metre of each line was put together out of shorter metrical units called *feet*, each with its own pattern of long and short syllables (**5.30**). The poems of Homer and Hesiod are 'epics' not in the first place because of their length or subject matter but for their metre, hexameter, which the Greek also called **epos**. The large majority of the epigrams of the Greek Anthology are in *elegiac couplets*, hexameter plus pentameter. The Christian epigrams of Book 1 are an exception: their typical metre is hexameters. But these were just two metres among many.

Book 13 is one of the Anthology's shortest. Unlike most other books, it contains poems on a variety of themes. Instead what unifies it is metre, or rather, weirdness in metre. These are the Anthology's 'polymetric' epigrams, poems written to show off unusual metres or combinations of metres, each with an explanatory caption. My translations do not attempt to replicate the features that made the book so distinctive.

Two of these three epigrams concern works of art, one of them dedicated to Hermes, the messenger of the gods whom the Romans called Mercury, and the other set up as a memorial to a much-missed friend. The Anthology must once have contained many more epigrams on works of art, including a whole book of them in regular elegiacs. Unfortunately that book is lost from the Palatine manuscript that is our best source for the Anthology, but some of its contents reach us through a later and inferior manuscript version, rearranged and censored by a monk named Planudes Maximus at the end of the thirteenth century. Since the rediscovery of the Palatine manuscript the epigrams that appear in Planudes but not in the Palatine have been gathered together into the so-called Planudean Appendix, also called Book 16. Most of them are about works of art.

Lycon wrote comedies at Athens in the fourth century BC and was a hit with Alexander the Great; he is known to have won twice at the Lenaea, the winter dramatic festival to Dionysus at which only comedies were staged. Then as now, January was a month when people needed all the cheering up they could get.

13.7 Callimachus

Comic tetrameter

> Menoetias of Lyctus hung up here
> And captioned so his former archer-gear:
> 'Sarapis, please accept my gift to you,
> This bow with tips of horn, and quiver too,
> Presented as a gift of my free will;
> Men of Benghazi keep the arrows still.'

13.8 Theodoridas

Archilochean tetrameter

> As victor in the longer running-race,
> The speedy son of Aristomachus
> Brought home this cauldron hammered out of brass.

Two verse captions notionally written to accompany dedications in temples. Lyctus in Callimachus' day was an important city of Crete, often at war with its now more famous neighbour Knossos. This local rivalry was a sideshow to the frequent, large-scale warfare between the great powers of the eastern Mediterranean and western Asia. Alexander had created a vast empire in the East; when he died without a viable succession plan, his generals carved it up into spheres of influence and founded dynasties that spent the next several centuries doing their best to wipe each other out. The most successful of them all were the Ptolemies of Egypt (7.39), and Menoetias is retiring after a successful career as a mercenary who has fought for them under contract. He has made enough money that he will not be needing the tools of his trade anymore, so he offers them in thanks for his safekeeping to a compound Graeco-Egyptian god, Sarapis. Blending the Egyptian Osiris and Apis (the latter worshipped at Memphis as a living god in the form of a sacred bull) with aspects of several Greek deities, this syncretistic and still fairly new divinity was heavily promoted by Ptolemy I and his successors as a state cult that could bring their Egyptian and Greek subjects together. Clearly Menoetias has spent a sizeable portion of his career in Egypt and has grown to appreciate Sarapis' protection.

Menoetias' mercenary service has included his king's campaign to conquer an important coastal city of the kingdom of Cyrene (modern Libya). The Greeks knew the modern Benghazi as Hesperis (Callimachus' choice), Euhesperides, or later, Berenice. In the 320s BC a charismatic Spartan mercenary leader named Thibron briefly took over Cyrene and led a revolt that the Ptolemies promptly put down, so we can date the firing of Menoetias' arrows to within a year or two. Callimachus' epigram is effectively court propaganda and there is no reason to suppose a real Menoetias commissioned it, but there was plenty of work for soldiers of fortune of his type.

Benghazi's ancient name of Hesperis means City of Evening. It is by no means the only place on the northern African coast to combine a troubled modern history with a distinguished classical past. Compare 9.425, by the Christian Byzantine poet John Barbocallus, on a city devastated by fire and earthquake:

> I am a city pitiful, undone:
> I lie all tumbled with my civic dead,
> Unluckiest by far in all the world.
> Hephaestus took me from Poseidon's rout.
> How beautiful I was, and now am dust.
> You that pass by, bewail my sorry fate:
> Cry for Berytus that has been destroyed.

The Romans knew Berytus proverbially as *Berytus Nutrix Legum*, 'the Nurse of Laws', and it remained a famous centre of legal education (which by then was the main route into politics) under the Byzantines. The sea-god Poseidon was also the lord of earthquakes, propitiated by his worshippers as Earthshaker (**Ennosigaios**), and lame Hephaestus was god of fire and the smithy. John is concisely telling us that Berytus was shattered by an earthquake and the

211

ensuing fire took whatever was left. Nonetheless it was rebuilt. Indeed it is still there today under its ancient name, Beirut.

Theodoridas was a poet of Syracuse and probably active in the late third or second century BC, epigram's Hellenistic heyday. We know he liked playing around with unusual metres (compare **13.21**). The 'longer running-race' of his poem is the **dolikhos**, a race of about three miles held only at the Olympic Games. We know a few names of winners in Theodoridas' day out of sources such as Pausanias but 'son of Aristomachus' gets us nowhere, and anyway, Olympic victors were never awarded prizes with cash value. If the cauldron was ever real, which I highly doubt, its metal has probably been melted down and recast many times since.

13.14 Simonides

Hexameter followed by a pentameter and two trimeters, then another hexameter

> Dandes of Argos, sprinter, lies within,
> Whose feats brought glory to the horse-grazed plain
> That fathered him. His two Olympic wins,
> Isthmians three, fifteen at Nemea—
> And as for all his other victories,
> I do not have the time to tally them.

13.21 Theodoridas

Complete trimeter followed by dimeter from the pantomimic pentameter

> MNASALCAS of Plataeae has this tomb,
> The elegist, who from Simonides

Tore off a fragment of a single page
To serve as Muse. He echoed emptily,
Bombastically spouting dithyrambs,
But he is dead, so let us not throw stones;
That said, if he were living, he would puff
And swell his kettledrum with gushing stuff.

A funny, nasty epitaph for a fellow-poet. Mnasalcas came from Plataeae near Sicyon in the northern Peloponnese, not to be confused with the more famous Plataea near which the combined Greek land forces had crushed the Persian invasion force in 479. Nineteen of his epigrams survive in the Greek Anthology, including a literary epitaph for Hesiod (**7.54**). Here is another by him (6.254) that could be said to run along Simonidean lines:

The shield of Alexander, Phylleus' son,
I hang here as a holy offering
To lord Apollo of the golden hair.
Worn is my rim and tired by constant war,
Worn too my boss, but courage makes me shine,
Courage I earned in arming that brave man
Who set me here. From when I first was made,
I never have been worsted or outdone.

The dithyramb of classical Athens was a traditional choral song-and-dance in lyric metres, performed in competition alongside tragedy at the City Dionysia, but it was already proverbial for pretentious and longwinded language in Plato's day (fourth century BC), and that is the sense in which Theodoridas uses it here. His 'spouting dithyrambs' (**dithurambokhāna**) is a single long word that takes up a whole dimeter line. It is a *hapax* (see note on **7.23**) found nowhere else in ancient literature, and Theodoridas assuredly made it up for effect. In fact all his vocabulary here is notably grandiose, and he must have known his own poem was far more bombastic than anything Mnasalcas had written. My guess is that he is sending himself up and that the epitaph is meant affectionately, though poets' send-offs for their rivals could be viciously unfair. Here is Erycius (7.377) on Parthenius of Nicaea, who came to Rome as booty from the Mithridatic Wars and is said to have taught Virgil to speak and read Greek:

> Though under earth he lies, still tar with pitch
> Foul-mouthed PARTHENIUS for the bile he spewed
> A thousand times on the Pierians,
> And for his vile, polluted elegies.
> His journey into madness went so far,
> He said that Homer's *Odyssey* was 'mud';
> The *Iliad*, 'a thorn-bush'. For which crimes
> The gloomy Furies in mid-Cocytus
> Have put him in a choke-chain, like a dog.

13.22 Phaedimus

Complete trimeter followed by epode (heroic tetrameter), limping at the penultimate <syllable>

> Your bow, Lord Sniper, that you used to slay
> The mighty Giant: curb its cruelty,
> Nor open up the quiver of those darts
> That killed the wolves. Against these bachelors
> Let fly instead the arrow made for Love
> So that they may defend their fatherland,
> Courageous in the intimate embrace

Of younger boys: he kindles martial might,
Ever the very strongest of the gods
To glorify the foremost in the fight.
Melistion's, these gifts, unto the god
The Schoenians have worshipped, man and boy;
I pray you take them kindly and enjoy.

Reported also as the author of an epic, the third-century poet Phaedimus was probably only a minor presence in the *Garland* of Meleager, in whose list of enrolled epigrammatists he is placed very near the end. His name means 'Shining' and some of Homer's best heroes bear it as an epithet. His four surviving epigrams confirm that he liked experimenting with metres (compare **13.2**). In this one a character named Melistion appeals to Apollo, calling him Worker-from-afar (**Hekaërgos**) and describing his quiver as Wolf-slaying (**Lukoktonos**). These traditional epithets emphasize Apollo's power of killing at a distance and mysteriously (he was also the god of plague). The nature of Melistion's offering is not specified but we may imagine him hanging up his own bow and arrows in gratitude to the patron god of archery now that his own days of battle are done.

Unusually Melistion begs the god to use his unerring aim not to inflict death but to help the arrows of Erōs find their mark. The intended targets are unmarried young men (**ēitheoi**), and the aim is to make them fall in love with adolescent boys (**kouroi**) slightly younger than themselves. Late in the poem we find out the scene is set at Thebes (Schoenus is a village nearby) and everything falls into place: Phaedimus' epigram is about the famous Sacred Band, an elite strike force of 300 men composed entirely of pairs of **erastai** and **erōmenoi** made fearless by mutual devotion. They were living proof of the power of Erōs to inspire a courage greater than death ('he kindles martial might').

Plato and Xenophon both seem to allude to the Sacred Band in their versions of the *Symposium* (fourth century BC), and Plutarch (first century AD) characteristically supplies lots of antiquarian detail, explaining, for instance, what made it Sacred—oaths sworn between lover and beloved at the shrine of Iolaus, who in some versions was a favoured **erōmenos** of the mighty Heracles. Here is part of Plutarch's *Life of Pelopidas* in the classic translation of John Dryden:

> For men of the same tribe or family little value one another when dangers press; but a band cemented by friendship grounded upon love is never to be broken, and invincible; since the lovers, ashamed to be base in sight of their beloved, and the beloved before their lovers, willingly rush into danger for the relief of one another. Nor can that be wondered at since they have more regard for their absent lovers than for others present; as in the instance of the man who, when his enemy was going to kill him, earnestly requested him to run him through the breast, that his lover might not blush to see him wounded in the back.

For Plutarch this army of lovers was ancient history: it had been wiped out at the Battle of Chaeronea by the Macedonian forces of Philip and his son Alexander (the future 'the Great') in 338 BC, long before even Phaedimus' day. Probably it had existed for less than a century, but, buoyed by Philip's praise ('Perish any man who suspects that these men either did or suffered anything that was base'), it went on to a mighty afterlife. The Sacred Band or 'Theban Legion' was taken up in the nineteenth century by early defenders of what we would now call gay rights, men such as John

Addington Symonds, a beloved and bestselling author on travel, art history, and Greek poetry. He delicately describes a time-honoured 'Dorian chivalry' of pair-bonded knights and squires:

> Heracles was the Eponym and patron of a [knightly] order which existed throughout Dorian Hellas. This order, protected by religious tradition and public favour, produced the Cretan lovers, the Lacedaemonian 'hearers' and 'inspirers', the Theban immortals who lay with faces turned so staunchly to their foes that vice seemed incompatible with so much valour. Achilles was another Eponym of this order.

Symonds was a sly propagandist and master of subtext, but his worship of Dorian chivalry was entirely sincere: it echoes in poems the public never saw, such as 'Eudiades' (*c.*1868):

> . . . Do ye believe—dull generations, dead
> In the cold mire of ignorance and dread—
> Do ye believe the pure and lofty love
> That stirred these children of the seed of Jove? . . .
> In vain. I faint. Yet listen, and endure:
> The men of whom I speak were strong and pure.
> No shame oppressed them: they could fight and fall;
> And the whole earth mourned at their funeral.

13.23 Asclepiades

Tetrameter made from a complete trimeter with the addition of a concluding **basis***, followed by tapering [lit. mouse-tailed] trimeter*

> Though you be pressed for time, o passer-by,
> Listen however briefly to the tale

Of Botrys and his overwhelming woe:
Eighty years old, he buried here his boy,
An infant, but his babble made some sense,
Already showed capacity. I cry
Not just for Botrys but for his dear son,
Robbed of life's pleasures when he was undone.

Every parent wants to feel their child is special. Infant mortality was rife in antiquity, and the Anthology has plenty of epitaphs for children—and for mothers who died giving birth to them (**7.167**). Here a father's grief is all the more acute because he has waited so very long. To reach eighty was unusual and to father a child at such an age, extraordinary; Botrys now knows he will die heirless, with no child to tend his own grave in time to come. In reflection of his suffering, he has commissioned an epitaph that cannot bear to name the boy he has lost—or at least, that is the scenario that Asclepiades has conjured up.

The boy was so young when he died that there is very little the poet can really say about him, but there is another pressing reason for his epitaph to be brief: it addresses whatever traveller is passing by on the road alongside which tombs were typically sited (**7.17**). Inscribed funerary epigrams know their readers have miles to go before they sleep; they must capture attention quickly and evoke sentiment before the audience has turned its head and moved on. Literary funerary epigrams inherit the inscriptional trope and face their own, analogous challenge. Their readers are not walking a stone-paved road, but they are nonetheless on the move, down the columns of a papyrus book-roll in which every poem is competing for their attention as they pass by. This epitaph grabs the reader right away—'Listen!'—and ends with the arresting trope of the inscribed stone itself shedding tears for these two connected lives, one ruined at its end, the other cut short before it had even really begun.

The bereaved father has a countryside kind of name. A **botrus** is a bunch of grapes, hence the botrytis fungus, the noble rot that makes for great dessert wines.

13.24 Callimachus

Last two feet of a tetrameter, followed by hendecasyllable

The gifts to Aphrodite offered here
Are Simo's, girl who wandered on the hill.
A portrait of herself; the belt that kissed
Her breasts when yet unwed; the fiery torch
And thyrsi that she waved in time before,
When she was crazy on the mountainside.

13.25 Callimachus

Two feet doubled, then tetrameter epode, running to one syllable more than a hexameter

Demeter of the Gate, in this her shrine
Built by Acrisius the Pelasgian:
To her and to her daughter underground
Did Timodēmus, man of Naucratis,
Leave as a gift one-tenth of profit made;
For this had been the nature of his vow.

Two by Callimachus, one of the first literary epigrammatists. The first is written as if to accompany a dedication in a temple of Aphrodite, goddess of sexuality and procreation. Simo's **zōna** (the original of our word 'zone') was a broad belt or girdle worn by unmarried young women, or in Greek, **parthenoi**. The Gospels describe Mary as a **parthenos**, and the Parthenon in Athens is so called because it is dedicated to Athena, a goddess with no interest in romantic relationships.

Simo he has no use for her **zōna** anymore because she is getting married. She used to be a Bacchant, a female devotee of Dionysus. Bacchants assembled in the wild, high places outside the city to lose themselves in worship of the god of wine and ecstasy—which literally means standing outside oneself (**ek-stasis**). You may recognize *ek/ex*, 'out of', and its close kin **exō**, 'outside of', from English words such as synecdoche, exoskeleton, or ekphrasis, the detailed description in literature (literally the 'talking-out') of a work of art (**5.185**). Latin used *ex* to mean the exact same thing, and our word exit is Latin for 'he/she goes out'.

Also known as *Maenads*, 'Crazy Ones', the Bacchants embraced their animal nature by dressing in fawn skins. They brandished **thursoi** (Latini *thyrsi*) sticks of giant fennel woven around with ivy (**6.312**), as they performed their mysterious rituals. Euripides wrote a brilliant tragedy, the *Bacchae*, with Dionysus as its star and Maenads as its chorus. Maenadism was sexy and scary, and a Maenad hanging up her dancing gear became a hit with Hellenistic poets. Here is another, anonymous example (**6.172**):

> Woman of Cnidus, Porphyris, now leaves
> Her double thyrsus that is like a spear,
> Garlands and anklet, wearing which she raved
> And footloose wandered Dionysus' way,
> An ivied fawnskin pinned across her breast.

For your own self, before your temple porch,
She sets aloft these her insignia,
Emblems of beauty and insanity.

The Temple of Demeter Amphictyonis was at Anthele, the village
neighbouring the 'Hot Gates' of Thermopylae; a Panhellenic
religious council called the 'Amphictyonic League' met there
every autumn. Some sources said the League had been founded
by Acrisius, a legendary king of Argos and the father of Danäe.
Demeter was the goddess of grain and agricultural fertility; she
is literally the Earth-Mother. Her daughter was Persephone,
whom Hades, god of the Underworld, abducted to be his bride.
The deal he then struck with her mother, by which Persephone
returned to the world above for six months of every twelve, sup-
plied the Greeks with their myth of the seasons. Persephone
was widely worshipped as Korē, the Maiden. Initiates of her
mysteries at Eleusis in Attica were forbidden ever to speak of
the revelations they had received from the revered goddess of
nature and death.

Trading by sea has taken Timodemus far from his home in
Naucratis. A river port on the Canopic branch of the Nile south
of Alexandria, it had been an important Greek mercantile base
in Egypt since archaic times. Herodotus (2.134–5) says it was
famous for its courtesans. Sappho's merchant brother Charaxus
sailed there from Lesbos and fell expensively in love with a local
girl called Rhodōpis. Timodemus' thank-offering of a tithe (one-
tenth of his profit) is a fairly standard amount to have vowed in
return for safety and success.

13.26 Simonides

The same tetrameter, followed by broken trimeter

> I shall remind: for it would not be right
> For her to rest here dead without a name,
> Splendid Xanthippe, Archenautes' wife,
> Whose great-great-grandsire once upon a time,
> Lord Periander, led the citizens
> In high-towered Corinth where he was the king.

13.27 Phalaecus

Tetrameter followed by complete trimeter, then alternating hexameter

> Phōcus has perished in an unknown place:
> His ship did not survive the darkened wave,
> Could not resist, descended far below
> The wide Aegean when the south-west wind
> Shredded the sea. And in his fathers' land
> His only portion is an empty tomb;
> His mother circles it, and shares the fate
> Of that unhappy bird, the halcyon.
> Each day Promēthis cries for her dear son,
> How long before his time he came undone.

Periander was tyrant of Corinth in the late sixth century and led it to the economic dominance that it enjoyed thereafter until the Roman sack of 146 BC; he was often counted among the Seven Sages. Greeks likes things in sevens as much as we do (deadly sins, samurai . . .): compare the Seven Wonders of the Ancient World. There was occasional disagreement as to which Wonders should be on the list, but never any doubt that there needed to be seven of them.

The Alcyone of myth drowned herself when her husband Ceyx was lost at sea; the pitying gods transformed the pair into halcyons, that is to say, kingfishers. Phalaecus must have a slightly different version of the story in mind. This Hellenistic epigrammatist was an innovator who developed a new metre for satirical verse, subsequently named Phalaecian in his honour. These lines of eleven syllables (hendecasyllables) then became famous as the preferred metre of the Latin poet Catullus, and are popular in Italian poetry to this day. In this epigram, though, Phalaecus mixes up other metres entirely.

Sea travel had obvious dangers, and writers of funerary epigram became fascinated by the literary problem of how to write an epitaph when there was no body to bury (**9.52**).

13.30 Simonides

Hexameter, and the same text as trochaic tetrameter by changing word order

Alcmene of the pretty ankles, Muse;
Sing me her son. Sing me the son, o Muse,
Of Alcmene whose ankles were so fine.

13.31 Timocreon

Echoing him

Some foolish stuff from Chios came my way,
And uninvited. Out of Chios came
Some foolishness that I did not invite.

BOOK 14

PUZZLES AND RIDDLES

14.20

If in the middle of a blazing fire
You place one hundred, you will find the one
That killed a maiden and was maiden's son.

14.21

If in the midst of lord Hephaestus' flame
You cast one hundred, you will find the one
That killed a maiden and was maiden's son.

'Answer: Pyrrhus, son of Deidamia, and slayer of Polyxena. If **rho**, the sign for 100, is inserted into the middle of the word **puros** (fire), it becomes **purrhos**'—so wrote William Paton, the tireless scholar who translated the whole Greek Anthology into English (with the very rude bits going into Latin instead) for the Loeb Classical Library in the 1910s. He did not have a high opinion of the book of riddles, but he stuck with it and offered

A Book of Greek Life: The Ancient World Through Epigram. Gideon Nisbet, Oxford University Press.
© Gideon Nisbet 2026. DOI: 10.1093/oso/9780198994756.003.0009

solutions where he could. You will recall that the letters of the Greek alphabet are also used to represent numbers: alpha is one, beta is two, and so on (**5.126**). 'Maiden' is **parthenos**, from which we get Parthenon and parthenogenesis (**13.25**).

This was clearly a popular riddle, since it comes down to us in two versions. Its mythical Pyrrhus shares only a name with the historical Macedonian king whose wars against Rome gave us the phrase 'Pyrrhic victory'. The name means 'fiery' and is for his red hair. The same Greek root gives us pyre and pyromaniac, and fool's gold is properly called pyrite, because it emits sparks when struck.

Also called Neoptolemus, this Pyrrhus was the son of Achilles. He came to Troy late in the war and participated in the slaughter, butchering King Priam's daughter Polyxena as a human sacrifice (something of which Greeks never approved) upon his father's tomb. So Polyxena is the maiden he killed; but of which maiden was he the son? The answer is surprising: the maiden is his father. Achilles' mother Thetis (herself a minor goddess) foresaw that a great war was coming and hid her adolescent son at the court of Lycomedes, king of Scyros, *disguised as a young woman*, so that he would not be called on to fight in it. Under the name 'Pyrrha', the disguised Achilles repaid Lycomedes' hospitality by sleeping with his daughter and getting her pregnant. Pyrrhus was the result. Eventually Odysseus came calling and caught him out.

The 'blazing fire' of the first line echoes a formula familiar from the *Iliad*. Homer's epics emerged from an oral epic tradition that spun great songs out of trained memory and a narrative technique of building-blocks: as well as characteristic epithets for characters such as 'swift-footed' for Achilles and 'lord of men' for Agamemnon (**5.30**), these included a repertoire of stock phrases and descriptions. Sunrises, for instance, are always described in the same terms; and heroes put on their armour in pretty much the same way each time, a way that makes sense—greaves first, while it's still easy to bend over. Troy is right by the sea but nobody in the *Iliad* eats fish because fish is insufficiently heroic for the kind of poem it is; instead the besieging Greeks seem to live on meat, specifically kebabs (**6.171**), which they prepare and cook in *exactly the same way*, every single time. After a few weeks of that, any of us would be ready to go on a killing spree.

14.22

Say nothing, and you say my proper name;
But if you have to speak, and here's the rub,
You say what people call me just the same.

14.28

From sea I draw a fishy parentage;
A single contest guarantees I come
To celebrate the Dionysia;
And when I ventured to the stadium,
And made my body slick with olive oil,
With my own hands I slew Demeter's son.
A second point of note: that I emit
A multitude of Giants from each side,
And they are hauled away by many hands.

14.35

> I am a part of man, that iron cuts,
> And cutting off a letter sets the sun.

The first of these riddles is a classic, and its answer is silence; you need know no Greek, and nothing of Greek culture, to work that one out.

A person *does* need Greek to solve the third riddle. Paton cracked it: the 'part of man that iron cuts' is a finger- or toenail, **onux**. The semi-precious stone onyx is so called because its banded patterning can resemble that of human nails. Taking off the first letter from **onux** leaves **nux**, meaning night. Raccoons are of the genus nyctereutēs, meaning night-wanderer, and nyctophiles like to be in the dark. The Latin close equivalent, *nox*, gives us nocturnal.

Paton did not hit upon the solution of the second riddle, but Professor Armand d'Angour has worked it out:

Tragos is a type of fish.

Tragos means 'goat', the nominal prize for tragedy at the Dionysia.

A goat, sacrificed at the Games (**stadion** = running race), was anointed in oil and sprinkled with barley (= Plutus, son of Demeter).

Tragos also means 'merchant-ship', which was rowed with 100 'giant' oars extending from its sides and 'hauled away by many hands'.

Whoever put this second riddle together expected their readers to work hard for their answer, but that is true of many of the puzzles of Book 14. Many of them are numerical challenges that were much trickier then than now. Paton introduces them with the following sniffy note:

> The problems . . . can be easily solved by *algebra*. The Scholiast gives somewhat cumbersome *arithmetical* solutions.

I have emphasized those two terms because they have very different roots. Arithmetic is from **arithmos**, the ancient Greek word for number, and Greek arithmetic was limited both by a cumbersome system of notation and by their reluctance to adopt a number we take for granted: zero, a concept of ancient Indian origin that comes to us wearing an Arabic name by way of Venice. Contrarily, the *al-* of algebra signals a word of Arabic origin; compare albatross, alchemy, alcohol, and alkali. At least one Greek mathematician was working on what would one day be called algebraic equations in the late Roman Empire (Diophantus, third century AD) but his method never caught on in the Graeco-Roman tradition. In time it was forgotten; the anonymous Byzantine scholar who added marginal comments to the Anthology's surviving manuscript was working out his sums in the same way his ancestors had, a thousand years earlier and more. Christendom was to wait another two centuries for the first translations of this marvellous infidel knowledge.

The Baghdadi mathematicians who perfected algebra probably knew Diophantus' works. A great deal of Greek scientific literature was translated into Arabic and often survives only in those translations. Unless they know Arabic, a classicist who wishes to read (say) an ancient Greek medical work must often access it at third hand, in a Latin translation of the Arabic translation of the lost Greek original.

14.40

There are two sisters in one family:
One sister births the other, and in turn
Is born from that same sister. So we learn
These two are sisters and of self-same kind,
Sister and mother each to her own line.

14.64

The Riddle of the Sphinx

There is an animal that walks the earth
On two legs, four, or even sometimes three,
But has a single name. Alone of beasts
That creep on land or move through sky or sea,
It changes nature. Yet its gait is least
Each time its count of legs is most increased.

14.97

Delphic oracle

When comes the time a man of foreign tongue
Shall yoke the sea with tree-bark, take good care
And keep your bleating he-goats from the fray;
Give up Euboea, and be far away.

The first of these riddles is fairly easy to solve: the two sisters are day (**hēmera**, the root of our 'ephemeral') and night (**nux**), both of them feminine nouns in Greek. All nouns in Greek are gendered masculine, feminine, or neuter (**5.137**), in a system that overlaps with, but extends far beyond, biological sex and social gender roles.

Announced by its subtitle, the second riddle is legend made verse. Imported into the myths of the Greeks from Egyptian lore, the Sphinx who terrorized Thebes set an impossible riddle to all challengers and ate them when they failed to solve it (her name means 'Constrictor'; we get sphincter from the same Greek root). Then came a wanderer called Oedipus (**9.167**) who realized the answer, saved the city, and became its new king, with the messy long-term consequences that so fascinated Freud.

The third riddle is an oracle. Confusingly in English we use that word both of the prophesying authority (in this instance the Oracle of Delphi, most hallowed of all the Greek oracles) and of the prophecies they issued to petitioners. Book 14 of the Anthology contains dozens of epigrams (poems 65–100) purporting to be oracles issued by these . . . oracles. The sanctuary's priests tidied up the inspired utterances of the Delphic priestess (the Pythia, **6.10**) into verse for their generously tipping customers, so some poems in the sequence are likely genuine. Others will have been made up by later authors who reckoned this was what the Oracle of Wherever really *ought* to have said when asked about a particular legendary or historic situation. This particular prediction is an interesting instance of editorial misfiling: it is *not* from Delphi, but from a Boeotian oracle called Bakis who we know was active at the time of the Persian Wars (**6.285**, **7.39**). Herodotus recorded it as part of his history of that conflict and the Anthology's compiler got it from there, fourteen hundred years or so later.

This poem in hexameters is the last of a series of six oracles (14.92–7) in the Anthology that were solicited by anxious Greek city-states when they heard Xerxes was on his way. What were they supposed to do, in the face of such overwhelming force? Bakis and the Delphic Oracle were in full agreement: any resistance against the god-king was doomed. That the Greeks beat the odds and triumphed was a big blow to the prediction-mongers' prestige.

BOOK 15

MISCELLANEOUS POEMS

15.11 <Aglochartus>

On the castle of Lindos

> Wide was the glory of that ancient town,
> Lindus, when it received Atrytone
> Upon its citadel that slopes to sky;
> And wider was its worldly fame again
> When swelled with that maid's favours, olive-green.
> To those who see its fertile crags today
> The place cries out it is Athena's home,
> A thriving one, for Aglochartus, priest,
> Set up this lovely gift at his own cost,
> More skilled than Celeus and Icarius
> At raising yield in olive through the land.

Book 15 of the Anthology is titled **Summikta**, Miscellaneous. What seems to be meant by this not very helpful title is that Cephalas mixed together epigrams he had found for himself, odd bits and pieces from outside the usual suspects (the anthologists Meleager, Philip, and Agathias; the individual poets Lucillius,

A Book of Greek Life: The Ancient World Through Epigram. Gideon Nisbet, Oxford University Press.
© Gideon Nisbet 2026. DOI: 10.1093/oso/9780198994756.003.0010

Strato, Gregory, and Palladas). He had probably done the same with the Christian epigrams of Book 1, and a lot of the epigrams in this book too are written by his Christian contemporaries.

This poem obviously is not. It is a genuine cult inscription that you can still see carved on a rock at Lindos on Rhodes, commemorating the planting of a grove of olive-trees in honour of Athena Atrytone ('Unwearied') by her green-fingered priest. Perhaps Cephalas visited the place and happened upon it, or maybe his friend Constantine of Rhodes (**15.18**) sent it his way as a local curiosity. Before the old gods were put out to grass, Lindos had been an ancient and world-famous centre of Athena's worship; celebrities such as Alexander the Great visited to pay her homage, and to hold a priesthood there was a prestigious honour that probably ran in Aglochartus' family. There are olive trees in the sanctuary of Athena Lindia to this day, and I would like to think that some are descended from his originals.

Athena took a special interest in the cultivation of olives, and the word that Cyrus uses to describe their colour, **glaukos**, is part of her Homeric epithet **glaukōpis**, meaning grey-eyed. Or perhaps it means blue-eyed, or green-, or shimmering-; we find **glaukos** in contexts that suggest one or more of these four. Greeks and Romans had the same eyes and brains as us, but they categorized and experienced visual effects such as colour differently. We confidently break up the spectrum into ROYGBIV, red-orange-yellow-etc., but nothing was orange until explorers brought back oranges and Europeans started talking about them. Before then, 'orange' things were either red or yellow, and ancient Romans didn't exactly have yellow either. They had blond(e) flavus—but that word described not just light-coloured hair, but the silty waters of the River Tiber.

The same Homeric epics that call Athena **glaukōpis** also famously describe the sea as **oinops**, found often in the line-ending formula **oinopa ponton**. The conventional translation into English is 'wine-dark', but all the Greek says is that the sea is 'wine-looking', that it looks like wine. Is it something about how the surface moves, about how the light hits it at a particular time of day, about how its horizon looks a bit like the meniscus in a shallow wine-cup held by lamplight? Your guess is as good as anyone else's.

The word Aglochartus uses for castle is **kastron**, a loan-word from Latin, where *castrum*—legionary fortress—is a word familiar to generations of students who sweated through Caesar's *Commentaries*.

15.18 Constantine of Rhodes

On the draughtboard

> They should have sawn your bones up, slice by slice,
> To make them pieces in your game of war,
> Since, Palamedes, you were in the wars
> And added yet another you had found,
> A war of friends on wooden battle-ground.

Constantine of Rhodes was an important friend of Cephalas, known for big, serious poetry: his imperially aggrandizing *On Constantinople and the Church of the Holy Apostles* is much discussed by scholars. He also wrote epigrams, and Cephalas put several into Book 15. Generally they are religious; this is an exception.

Chess with its knights and castles is obviously modelled on war, and so was its precursor. A famous black-figure vase by Exekias (mid-sixth century BC) in the British Museum shows the rival Greek heroes Achilles and Ajax bent over a game board in full armour. (It is conventional to say 'vase', but nobody put flowers in them: these vessels were amphorae, made for bringing wine to table at the symposium, where Homerically literate guests feasted in heroic style.) In real war nothing happens a lot of the time, and the heroes are occupying time during a lull by simulating war using Palamedes' new invention. Exekias adds captions that make Achilles say 'four', and Ajax 'three'—these must be their scores, so Achilles is winning (Ajax was a strong fellow but not bright). Neither hero lived to see the real game won.

The Greek credited Palamedes with various inventions besides draughts or checkers: dice for gaming; maybe the numbers with which they did their sums; and probably some letters of the alphabet. None of this is historically real; the Greeks enjoyed attributing the skills (**tekhnai**) of civilization to various legendary figures. Their word for such a person or demigod was **prōtos heuretēs** or 'first finder'. Daedalus, for instance, was the first finder of sculpture but also (depending on who you asked) of woodworking and the sailing ship; Aristaeus discovered beekeeping. Palamedes outdid them all in cleverness: he even outtricked the master trickster, Odysseus, who would otherwise have avoided taking part in the Trojan War at all. Odysseus never forgave him and eventually engineered his death, in one version (and there were several) by framing him for treason. None of this is in Homer, but Exekias knew his would meet diners who knew *all* the stories.

As well as gambling with dice and knucklebones the Greeks and Romans enjoyed a range of board games, and enough boards survive (carved for instance into the counters of wine bars) to encourage gamer classicists to recreate likely versions of the rules and post them online. Romans played a draughts-like game called *latrunculi* ('bandits') on a gridded board that was probably more or less Palamedes' **tabla**. They also knew early versions of backgammon and noughts-and-crosses. Romans associated gaming and gambling with bad characters: soldiers and slaves. They were morally dangerous activities that were liable to lead to violence. Officially gambling was banned except during the winter carnival of Saturnalia, though that hardly stopped anyone. Constantine's sadistically pious wish to see Palamedes' bones sectioned into draughts pieces is therefore not so much a Christian denunciation of sin (though Christians disapproved of gambling too) as old-fashioned aristocratic disdain for the lower pleasures.

15.21 <Theocritus>

The Syrinx of Theocritus

> The wife who slept with No-one, and whose son was the Far-fighter,
>   birthed another one,
> A swift director of the nurse for whom a stone was swapped, and not
>   the horned,
> Whom once the ox-born succoured, but whose heart a shield's rim,
>   minus 'P'
> Once set alight. By birth-name he is Whole, but of two natures,
> Who yearned for the Meropian voice-born girl, the breezy one;

Who crafted high-pitched harm, a testament of fiery love,
For Muse with violet crown; who stemmed the force like-named
To his grandfather-slayer, freeing too the girl
Who came from Tyre. Paris Simichidas
Gave him this prized possession of
The blind-bearers. Delighting in
Your soul at it, flock-mounter,
Saettians' goad, thief-sired
Sireless, box-footed,
May you pipe sweet
To the mute girl,
Calliope,
Unseen.

This overly clever poem is addressed to the god Pan, to whom the poet Theocritus (also called Simichidas) offers shepherd's pipes on which to play music, but you would need several degrees to work that out. Luckily for me I had Paton's old, public-domain Loeb, where you may find it all explained if you really want (**Introduction, p. 9**). The allusions are wilfully obscure—the epitome of Hellenistic showing-off, in a generation of scholar-poets drunk on the new possibilities in information retrieval opened up by the Library of Alexandria (**7.17**).

I will limit myself to just two of them. The first is relatively easy, found in the very first line and accessible to anyone who knows Homer's *Odyssey* or stories based on it. Odysseus escapes the cave of the Cyclops Polyphemus by means of a cunning plan (his speciality) that involves persuading his captor that his name is Nobody; when he blinds the Cyclops and breaks out, Polyphemus' cries of 'Nobody is hurting me!' do not bring the other Cyclopes running.

The second is Pan's name, hidden four lines down in 'By birth-name he is Whole'. Probably by accident, the name of Pan is identical to the neuter form of the Greek adjective meaning 'all' or 'every', **pas–pasa–pan**. This adjective comes through into various compound words in English. Consider a pandemic, something that affects all the people—the -demic bit is from **dēmos**, the citizen body as a whole, also found in our democracy (rule by the people) and demographics (writing about the people). A panacea would cure a pandemic and every other ailment too, helping avoid pandemonium—which is literally all hell let loose. Just as well, because pandemonium would cause widespread panic, and *that* is not from 'all/every' but from Pan himself—panic is the state of ecstasy (literally 'standing outside oneself') into which his followers enter during his worship.

Isn't the shape peculiar? My translation does its best to mimic what Theocritus is doing. He made each line shorter, dropping syllables along the way, so that his poem not only *describes* a set of Pan-pipes but is also *shaped like* them. The *Syrinx* is the first and most famous of the Anthology's sequence of pattern-poems, so called. The remainder (15.22 and 24–7) pull the same trick with an axe, the wings of Erōs, two altars (relatively easy), and an egg.

In myth, Syrinx was a nymph (water-spirit) whom Pan desired to take as a lover. She fled, changing into reeds in a stream. Pan cut them to make a new musical instrument, the pipes. Myth is not nice. The story hangs together more tightly than an English telling shows: the Greek word for reed is **syrinx**. The same term is used for various narrow tubes and channels, from a pore in the lungs to the firing groove of a bolt-thrower and the passage-tomb of a bygone Pharaoh. From its third-declension (**6.254**) stem we get our English word, *syringe*.

15.44

On Porphyrius the Charioteer

> Porphyrius had set aside his toil,
> Put off his belt. He stood here once before
> In bronze to mark his excellence, and now
> He stands again in bronze and silver too.
> Old man, sent honours from a far-off shore,
> You heard the people shouting, and once more
> Took up your whip, and now again you rage
> Upon the track as if of half your age.

The Colosseum (built in the 70s AD, and 'Flavian Amphitheatre' if we're being technical) was all well and good, but Rome's greatest sporting venue was always the Circus Maximus. Much older and much bigger, this was the venue for chariot racing between factions (teams)—the Reds, Whites, Blues, and Greens—that inspired passionate followings. The empire's Greek subjects never took to gladiatorial shows, but they had always loved racing (**5.147, 7.34–5**) and the circuses at Antioch and Constantinople were epic in scale and magnificence (Antioch is the setting for the fictional chariot-race in the novel *Ben-Hur* and its many adaptations). Long after Christianity had retired the gladiatorial *munera*—and it took its time about it—the Circus remained the beating heart of Byzantium's capital.

This epigram and its companions in the Anthology (15.41–51) captioned real statues of famous racers erected along the central spine of the racetrack: a couple of their bases have been found, with the inscriptions in place. Porphyrius ('Purple') was the greatest sporting star of them all. Born in Libya and beginning his career as a young man at the end of the fifth century AD, he raced at Constantinople and other great Byzantine cities too, moving between factions as he amassed wealth and fame. It was a young man's game and a very dangerous one. Porphyrius made his fortune and retired, being granted an honorific statue to mark his illustrious career—only to be lured back out of retirement and race to glory yet again. So when he retired for good, definitely calling it quits this time, the statue had to be redone in acknowledgement of *two* illustrious careers.

Hot on the heels of Porphyrius' retirement a whale (probably a big orca) started terrorizing shipping in the vicinity of Constantinople, probably for the fun of it, and kept it up for more than fifty years. Sailors nicknamed it Porphyrius. Nobody is quite sure why, but it is nice to think that homage to the great charioteer is somewhere in the mix. The whale Porphyrius is in both of Procopius' histories—the Secret one, and the not-so-secret—and has its own Wikipedia page. Modern news stories about boat-bothering orcas have made it a celebrity again, outshining its charioteer namesake.

MELEAGER'S CODA

And so we draw to a close. The following two poems (12.256–7) concluded the erotic book of Meleager's *Garland*, and the *Garland* as a whole. In terms of art each is a *sphragis* (seal). The metaphor is of an author stamping his mark as with a signet-ring in wax. There can be no better way to put *A Book of Greek Life* to bed. Both translations first appeared in my World's Classics *Epigrams from the Greek Anthology*.

The word I translate THE END in the second epigram is **korōnis**, a marginal mark that marked a major break in a text or more usually its end. As the Latinized *coronis* it has its own Unicode symbol (U+2E0E). The Greek for crow is **korōnē** and some early versions of the symbol look quite bird-like; later it became more of a helical squiggle. It therefore looked quite 'like a serpent coil', and so of course did the book-roll that it concluded.

> Cypris, for you this garland Love did weave,
> Containing every blossom that he plucked;
> A wreath of boys to cozen every heart.
> Therein he plaited Diodorus sweet,
> A lily, and therein Asclepiades,

A Book of Greek Life: The Ancient World Through Epigram. Gideon Nisbet, Oxford University Press.
© Gideon Nisbet 2026. DOI: 10.1093/oso/9780198994756.003.0011

A lovely wallflower; Heraclitus too
He wove atop them, rose amid the thorn,
And Diōn, like the bloom upon the vine;
Thērōn as well, a boy who flowered gold,
Saffron his hair; a sprig of Uliades,
The tufted thyme; Myiscus' tender leaves,
A shoot of olive that is evergreen;
And clipped the lovely boughs of Aretas.
The happiest of isles is holy Tyre,
That owns the scented grove where grow the blooms
Of boys that Aphrodite breathes upon.

I am THE END, and tell the waiting crowd
That now the race is at the final turn,
Most trusty guardian of the scripted scroll.
I say that he who gleaned from all the bards
And span their work together in this roll
Is *Meleager*: he completed it,
And wove this flower-wreath of minstrelsy
For Diocles, in lasting memory.
My whole lies wound here like a serpent coil;
I am enthroned beside his learning's end.

Thank you for your time.
END

INDEX

For the benefit of digital users, indexed terms that span two pages (e.g., 52–53) may, on occasion, appear on only one of those pages